Salvatore Maria Brandi

A Last Word on Anglican Ordinations

Salvatore Maria Brandi

A Last Word on Anglican Ordinations

ISBN/EAN: 9783337401252

Printed in Europe, USA, Canada, Australia, Japan

Cover: Foto ©Lupo / pixelio.de

More available books at **www.hansebooks.com**

A LAST WORD ON ANGLICAN ORDINATIONS

BEING AN EXPOSITION OF THE PONTIFICAL BULL
"APOSTOLICAE CURAE," CONTAINING A COMPLETE
REFUTATION OF ALL THE OBJECTIONS
RAISED AGAINST THE PAPAL
DECISION,

BY THE
REV. S. M. BRANDI, S. J.

ROME, (ITALY)

WITH A SPECIAL BRIEF FROM THE SOVEREIGN PONTIFF
APPROVING THE WORK,

AND NOTES BY THE
REV. SYDNEY F. SMITH, S. J.

LONDON, (ENGLAND.)

ONLY AUTHORIZED ENGLISH VERSION.
(COPYRIGHTED.)

The American Ecclesiastical Review,
NEW YORK.
1897.

The Last Word on the Subject of Anglican Orders from the Apostolic See.

Editor's Preface.

WHEN the Sovereign Pontiff, Leo XIII., made public his decisive answer to the question: *Whether the Catholic Church could accept as valid the Orders administered by the Bishops of the Anglican Establishment*, he spoke as the Supreme Judge in matters of Catholic faith, morals and discipline. That such a sentence should be final must be concluded not only from the historical evidence which supports it, but from the very character of the tribunal whence the decision proceeds. In truth Leo XIII. has only formulated the constant judgment of his predecessors in the Supreme Apostolic Office, and in doing so has summed up, in a more explicit manner than had previously been attempted, the evidence upon which that judgment necessarily rests.

Although the Bull *Apostolicæ Curæ*, which sets forth the reasons of the Papal decision, is complete and conclusive, inasmuch as it demonstrates the utter futility of the Anglican claims, it was not to be expected that the Pontiff in delivering a judicial decision would enter into each detail, and discuss separately the numerous arguments brought forth by those who cling to the contrary opinion. This task is of necessity reserved to apologists qualified to explain and illustrate, by reference to the sources of history and theology, whatever might require clearing up in the minds of those who are still

insufficiently informed to appreciate the full justice of the decision.

Such has been the work undertaken by the Rev. S. M. Brandi, to whom Leo XIII. himself has given the testimony that he has rightly understood, and aptly expressed the mind of the Sovereign Pontiff on this important question.

Father Brandi has taken each point of the Bull and elucidated it by logical argument and careful reference to the historical facts involved in the discussion. And since the Holy Father was from the beginning aware of the main purpose of Father Brandi's work he directed that the latter have free access to all the departments of the Holy Office and to the Secret Archives of the Vatican Library, in order that he might be able to utilize whatever documents could be found in addition to those already examined by the Papal Commission previously appointed for this purpose, whilst all the acts and arguments of this same special Commission were likewise at his disposal. In addition to the work of translation the Rev. Sydney F. Smith, S. J. (London), has subjoined to present edition his own notes, particularly valuable in view of much information gathered by him during the inquiry on the subject of Anglican Orders, in which he took a leading part.

No point of the discussion remains unnoticed and unanswered, and those who will take the trouble to read carefully the following pages will therein find a complete refutation of the arguments brought forth by Anglican writers in the past, and refurbished with modern phrase and assurance in the recent Letter of the Archbishops of Canterbury and of York addressed to the Catholic Clergy.

H. J. H.

APOSTOLIC LETTER ON ANGLICAN ORDINATIONS.

Leo Episcopvs

SERVVS SERVORVM DEI.

Ad Perpetuam Rei Memoriam.

Apostolicae curae et caritatis, qua *Pastorem magnum ovium, Dominum nostrum Iesum Christum* (¹), referre pro munere et imitari, aspirante eius gratia, studemus non exiguam partem pernobili Anglorum

1 Hebr. xiii. 20.

Leo, Bishop,

SERVANT OF THE SERVANTS OF GOD.

In Perpetual Remembrance.

We have given to the interests of the noble English nation no slight part of the Apostolic care and charity with which, aided by His grace, We endeavor to fulfill the office, and follow in the footsteps of the great Pastor of the flock, Our Lord Jesus Christ.

nationi tribuimus. Voluntatis in ipsam Nostrae ea praecipue testis est epistola quam superiore anno dedimus propriam *ad Anglos, regnum Christi in fidei unitate quaerentes:* eiusdem quippe gentis et veterem cum Ecclesia matre coniunctionem commemorando revocavimus, et felicem reconciliationem, excitatâ in animis orandi Dei sollertia, contendimus maturare. Rursusque haud ita pridem, quum communibus universe litteris de unitate Ecclesiae fusius agere visum est, non ultimo loco respeximus Angliam; spe praelucente, posse documenta Nostra tum catholicis firmitatem tum dissidentibus salutare lumen afferre. Atque illud fateri libet quod aeque gentis humanitatem ac multorum sollicitudinem salutis aeternae commendat, id est quam benevole Anglis probata sit instantia Nostra et dicendi libertas,

In the Letter, which last year We sent to the English seeking the Kingdom of Christ in unity of faith, We recalled the memory of the ancient union of that people with the Mother Church, and We strove to hasten the day of a happy reconciliation by stirring up men's hearts to offer anxious prayer to God. And again, more recently, when it seemed good to Us to treat more fully the unity of the Curch in a universal appeal, England had not the last place in Our mind in the hope that our teaching might both strengthen Catholics and bring the saving light to those separated from us. It is pleasing to acknowledge the generous way in which Our endeavor and openness of speech, inspired by no mere human motives, have met the approval of the English people, a fact which testifies not less to their nobilty of mind than to the solicitude of many for their eternal salvation.

With the same mind and intention We now purpose to turn Our thoughts to a

nullo quidem acta humanae rationis impulsu. Nunc autem eâdem Nos mente eodemque animo deliberatum habemus studia convertere ad quamdam non minoris momenti causam, quae cum ea ipsa re votisque Nostris cohaeret. Quod enim apud Anglos, aliquanto postquam ab unitatis christianae centro abscessum est, novus plane ritus ordinibus sacris conferendis, sub rege Eduardo VI., fuit publice inductus; defecisse idcirco verum Ordinis sacramentum, quale Christus instituit, simulque hierarchicam successionem, iam tenuit communis sententia, quam non semel Ecclesiae acta et constans disciplina firmarunt. Attamen recentiore memoria hisque maxime annis invaluit controversia, sacraene Ordinationes ritu eduardiano peractae, natura sacramenti effectuque polleant; faventibus, affirmate vel dubitanter, non modo scriptoribus anglicanis nonnullis, sed paucis etiam catholicis praesertim non Anglis. Alteros quippe matter of no less importance and closely connected with the same subject and with Our hopes. For an opinion already prevalent, confirmed more than once by the action and constant practice of the Church, maintained that when in England, shortly after it was rent from the centre of Christian unity, a new rite for conferring Holy Orders was publicly introduced under Edward VI., the true Sacrament of Orders as instituted by Christ lapsed, and with it the hierarchical succession. For some time, however, and in these last years especially, a controversy has sprung up as to whether the Sacred Orders conferred according to the Edwardine Ordinal possessed the nature and effect of a sacrament. In favor of the absolute validity were not only certain Anglican writers, but some few Catholics, chiefly non-English. The consideration of the excellency of the Christian priesthood moved Anglican writers in this matter, desir-

movebat praestantia sacerdotii christiani, exoptantes ut duplici eius in corpus Christi potestate ne carerent sui; movebat alteros consilium expediendi quodammodo illis reditus ad unitatem: utrisque vero hoc persuasum esse videbatur, iam studiis in eo genere cum aetate provectis, novisque litterarum monumentis ex oblivione erutis, retractari auctoritate Nostra causam non inopportunum fore. Nos autem ea consilia atque optata minime negligentes maximeque voci obsequentes apostolicae caritatis, censuimus nihil non experiri quod videretur quoquo modo conducere ad animarum vel avertenda damna vel utilitates fovendas.

Placuit igitur de retractanda causa benignissime indulgere: ita sane, ut per summam novae disquisitionis sollertiam, omnis in posterum vel species quidem dubitandi esset remota. Quapropter certo numero viris doctrina et eruditione praestantibus, quorum compertae erant dissimiles in

ous as they were that their own people should not lack the two-fold power over the Body of Christ. Catholic writers were impelled by a wish to clear the way for the return of Anglicans to holy unity. Both, indeed, thought that in view of studies fostered by the light of recent research, and of new documents rescued from oblivion, it was not inopportune to re-examine the question under the sanction of Our authority. And, We, not disregarding such desires and opinions, and, above all, obeying the dictates of Apostolic charity, thought that nothing should be left untried that might in any way tend to preserve souls from harm or procure their advantage.

It has, therefore, pleased Us to allow the cause to be re-examined, so that by reason of a most thorough examination, all doubt, even its least shadow, should be removed for the future. To this end We commissioned a certain number of men noted for their learning and ability, whose opinions in

Apostolic Letter.

ipsa causa opiniones, negotium dedimus ut momenta sententiae suae scriptis mandarent: eos deinde ad Nos accitos iussimus communicare inter se scripta, et quidquid eo amplius ad rem cognitu esset dignum, indagare atque expendere. Consultumque a Nobis est, ut ipsi diplomata opportuna omni possent copia in tabulariis vaticanis sive nota recognoscere sive inexplorata educere; itemque ut prompta haberent quaecumque eiusdem generis acta apud sacrum Consilium, quod *Suprema* vocatur, asservarentur, neque minus quaecumque ad hoc tempus doctiores viri in utramque partem evulgassent. Huiusmcdi adiumentis instructos, voluimus eos in singulares congressiones convenire; quae ad duodecim sunt habitae, praeside uno ex S. R. E. Cardinalibus a Nobis met ipsis designato, data singulis facultate disputandi libera. Denique earumdem congressionum acta, una cum ceteris documentis, Venerabilibus Fratribus Nostris

this matter were known to be divergent, to state the grounds of their judgments in writing. We then, having summoned them to Our presence, directed them to communicate the results of their inquiry to each other, and further to investigate and discuss whatever appeared requisite to obtain a full knowledge of the matter. We were careful also that they should be able to re-examine all documents bearing on this question which were known to exist in the Vatican archives; to search for new ones, and even to have at their disposal all acts relating to this subject which are adduced by learned men on both sides. We ordered them, when prepared in this way, to meet together in special sessions. These, to the number of twelve, were held under the presidency of one of the Cardinals of the Holy Roman Church, appointed by Ourselves, and all were invited to the freest discussion. Finally, We directed that the acts of

Cardinalibus ex eodem Consilio iussimus exhiberi omnia; qui meditata causa eaque coram Nobis deinde agitata, suam quisque sententiam dicerent.

Hoc ducendae rei ordine praestituto, ad intimam tamen aestimationem causae aequum erat non ante aggredi, quam id perstudiose quaesitum apparuisset, quo loco ea iam esset secundum Apostolicae Sedis praescriptiones institutamque consuetudinem; cuius consuetudinis et initia et vim magni profecto intererat reputare. Quocirca in primis perpensa sunt documenta praecipua quibus Decessores Nostri, rogatu reginae Mariae, singulares curas ad reconciliationem ecclesiae Anglicae contulerunt. Nam Iulius III. Cardinalem Reginaldum Pole, natione Anglum, multiplici laude eximium, Legatum de latere ad id opus destinavit, *tamquam pacis et dilectionis angelum suum*, eique mandata seu facultates extra ordinem

these meetings, together with all other documents, should be submitted to Our venerable brethren, the Cardinals of the same Council, so that when all had studied the whole subject and discussed it in Our presence, each might give his opinion.

This order for discussing the matter having been determined upon, it was necessary, with a view to forming a true estimate of the real state of the question, to enter upon it only after careful inquiry as to how the matter stood in relation to the prescription and settled custom of the Holy See, the origin and force of which custom it was undoubtedly of great importance to determine. For this reason, in the first place, the principal documents in which Our predecessors, at the request of Queen Mary, exercised their special care for the reconciliation of the English Church were considered. Thus Julius III. sent Cardinal Reginald Pole, an Englishman and

normasque agendi tradidit[1]; quas deinde Paulus IV. confirmavit et declaravit. In quo ut recte colligatur quidnam in se commemorata documenta habeant ponderis, sic oportet fundamenti instar statuere, eorum propositum nequaquam a re abstractum fuisse, sed rei omnino inhaerens ac peculiare. Quum enim facultates Legato apostolico ab iis Pontificibus tributae, Angliam dumtaxat religionisque in ea statum respicerent; normae item agendi ab eisdem eidem Legato quaerenti impertitae, minime quidem esse poterant ad illa generatim decernenda sine quibus sacrae ordinationes non valeant, sed debebant attinere proprie ad providendum de ordinibus sacris in eo regno, prout temporum monebant re-

[1] Id factum augusto mense MDLIII. per litteras sub plumbo, *Si ullo unquam tempore* et *Post nuntium Nobis*, atque alias.

illustrious in many ways, to be his Legate *de latere* for the purpose, *as his angel of peace and love*, and gave him special mandates or faculties, and directions for his guidance. These Paul IV. confirmed and explained. And here, to interpret rightly the force of these documents, it is necessary to lay it down as a fundamental principle that they were certainly not intended to deal with an abstract state of things, but with a specific and concrete issue. For, since the faculties given by these Pontiffs to the Apostolic Legate had reference to England only, and to the state of religion therein, and since the rules of action were laid down by them at the request of the said Legate, they could not have been mere directions for determining the necessary conditions for the validity of ordinations in general. They must pertain directly to providing for Holy Orders in the said kingdom as the recognized condition of the circumstances and times demanded. This, be-

rumque conditiones expositae. Hoc ipsum, praeter quam quod ex natura et modo eorumdem documentorum perspicuum est, inde pariter liquet, quod alienum prorsus fuisset, ita velle de iis quae sacramento Ordinis conficiendo necesse sunt, propemodum commonefieri Legatum, cumque virum cuius doctrina etiam in Concilio Tridentino eluxerat.

Ista probe tenentibus non difficulter patebit quare in litteris Iulii III. ad Legatum apostolicum, perscriptis die VIII. martii MDLIV., distincta sit mentio de iis primum qui *rite et legitime promoti*, in suis ordinibus essent retinendi, tum de iis qui *non promoti ad sacros ordines*, possent, *si digni et idonei reperti fuissent*, *promoveri*. Nam certe definiteque notatur, ut reapse erat, duplex hominum classis; hinc eorum qui 'sacram ordinationem vere suscepissent, quippe id vel ante Henrici secessionem, vel si post eam et per ministros errore dissidiove implicitos, ritu tamen catholico con-

sides being clear from the nature and form of the said documents, is also obvious from the fact that it would have been altogether irrelevant to thus instruct the Legate, one whose learning had been conspicuous in the Council of Trent, as to the conditions necessary for the bestowal of the Sacrament of Orders.

For those who justly estimate these facts it will not be difficult to understand why, in the letters of Julius III., issued to the Apostolic Legate on March 8, 1554, there is a distinct mention of, first, those who were *rightly and lawfully promoted* to Orders, and then, of others who, *not promoted to sacred orders*, might *be promoted if they were found to be worthy and fitting subjects*. For it is clearly and definitely noted, as indeed was the case, that there were two classes of men—first, those who had really received sacred Orders, either before the secession of Henry VIII., or, if after it, and by ministers infected by

Apostolic Letter.

sueto; inde aliorum qui initiati essent secundum Ordinale eduardianum, qui proterea possent *promoveri*, quia ordinationem accepissent irritam. Neque aliud sane Pontificis consilium fuisse, praeclare confirmat epistola eiusdem Legati, die XXIX. ianuarii MDLV., facultates suas episcopo Norwicensi demandantis. Id amplius est potissime considerandum quod eae ipsae Iulii III. litterae afferunt, de facultatibus pontificiis libere utendis, etiam in eorum bonum quibus munus consecrationis, *minus rite et non servata forma Ecclesiae consueta*, impensum fuit: qua quidem locutione ii certe designabantur qui consecrati eduardiano ritu; praeter eam namque et catholicam formam alia nulla erat eo tempore in Anglia.

Haec autem apertiora fient commemorando legationem quam Philippus et

error and schism, still according to the usual Catholic rite; second, those who were initiated according to the Edwardine Ordinal, who, therefore, were to be *promoted* since they had received an ordination which was null. And that the mind of the Pope was this and nothing else is clearly confirmed by the letter of the said Legate (January 29, 1555), sub-delegating his faculties to the Bishop of Norwich. Moreover, what the letters of Julius III. themselves say about freely using the Pontifical faculties, even in behalf of those who had received their consecration *not according to the rite and the accustomed form of the Church*, is to be especially noted. By this expression those only could be meant who had been consecrated according to the Edwardine rite, since besides it and the Catholic form there was then no other in England.

This becomes even still clearer when we consider the legation which, on the advice of Cardinal Pole,

Maria reges, suadente Cardinali Polo, Romam ad Pontificem februario mense MDLV. miserunt. Regii oratores, viri tres *admodum insignes et omni virtute praediti*, in quibus Thomas Thirlby, episcopus Eliensis, sic habebant propositum, Pontificem de conditione rei religiosae in eo regno notitia ampliore edocere, ab ipsoque in primis petere ut ea quae Legatus ad eiusdem regni cum Ecclesia reconciliationem curaverat atque effecerat, haberet rata et confirmaret: eius rei causâ omnia ad Pontificem allata sunt testimonia scripta quae oportebat, partesque Ordinalis novi proxime ad rem facientes. Iamvero Paulus IV. legatione magnifice admissa, eisdemque testimoniis per certos aliquot Cardinales *diligenter discussis*, et *habita deliberatione matura*, literas *Praeclara Carissimi* sub plumbo dedit die XX. iunii eodem anno. In his quum comprobatio plena et robur additum sit rebus a Polo gestis, de ordinationibus sic est praescriptum :... *qui ad or-*

the Sovereign Princes, Philip and Mary, sent to the Pope in Rome, in the month of February, 1555. The Royal Ambassadors, three men "most illustrious and endowed with every virtue," of whom one was Thomas Thirlby, Bishop of Ely, were charged to inform the Pope more fully as to the religious condition of the country, and especially to beg that he would ratify and confirm what the Legate had been at pains to effect, and had succeeded in effecting, towards the reconciliation of the Kingdom with the Church. For this purpose all the necessary written evidence, and the pertinent parts of the new Ordinal were submitted to the Pope. The Legation having been splendidly received, and their evidence having been diligently discussed by several of the Cardinals, after mature deliberation Paul IV. issued his Bull *Praeclara Carissimi*, on June 20, of that same year. In this, while giving full force and approbation to what Pole

dines ecclesiasticos... ab alio quam ab episcopo rite et recte ordinato promoti fuerunt, eosdem ordines... de novo suscipere teneantur. Quinam autem essent episcopi tales, *non rite recteque ordinati*, satis iam indicaverant superiora documenta, facultatesque in eam rem a Legato adhibitae: ii nimirum qui ad episcopatum, sicut alii ad alios ordines, promoti essent, *non servatâ forma Ecclesiae consueta*, vel non servata *Ecclesiae forma et intentione*, prout Legatus ipse ad episcopum Norwicensem scribebat. Hi autem non alii profecto erant nisi qui promoti secundum novam ritualem formam; cui quoque examinandae delecti Cardinales attentam operam dederant. Neque praetermittendus est locus ex eisdem Pontificis litteris, omnino rei congruens; ubi cum aliis beneficio dispensationis egentibus numerantur qui *tam ordines quam beneficia ecclesiastica nulliter et de facto obtinuerant. Nulliter* enim obtinuisse had done, it is ordered in the matter of the ordinations as follows: *Those who have been promoted to ecclesiastical Orders by any one but by a Bishop validly and lawfully ordained are bound to receive those Orders again;* but who those Bishops not *validly and lawfully ordained* were, had been made sufficiently clear by the foregoing documents, and the faculties used in the said matter by the Legate; those, namely, who have been promoted to the episcopate, as others to other Orders, *not according to the accustomed form of the Church*, or, as the Legate himself wrote to the Bishop of Norwich, *the form and intention of the Church* not having been observed. These were certainly those promoted according to the new form of rite, to the examination of which the Cardinals specially deputed had given their careful attention. Neither should a passage, much to the point, in the same Pontifical letter, be overlooked,

ordines idem est atque irrito actu nulloque effectu, videlicet *invalide*, ut ipsa monet eius vocis notatio et consuetudo sermonis; praesertim quum idem pari modo affirmetur de ordinibus quod de *beneficiis ecclesiasticis*, quae ex certis sacrorum canonum institutis manifesto erant nulla, eo quia cum vitio infirmante collata. Huc accedit quod, ambigentibus nonnullis quinam revera episcopi, *rite et recte ordinati*, dici et haberi possent ad mentem Pontificis, hic non multo post, die XXX. octobris, alias subiecit litteras in modum Brevis: atque, *Nos*, inquit, *haesitationem huiusmodi tollere, et serenitati conscientiae eorum qui schismate durante ad ordines promoti fuerant, mentem et intentionem quam in eisdem litteris Nostris habuimus clarius exprimendo, opportune consulere volentes, declaramus eos tantum episcopos et archiepiscopos qui non in forma Ecclesiae ordinati et consecrati fuerunt, rite et recte ordinatos dici non posse.* Quae de- where, together with others needing dispensation, are enumerated those *who had obtained as well Orders as benefices "nulliter et de facto."* For to obtain orders *nulliter* means that they are an act null and void, that is invalid, as the very meaning of the word and as common usage of language require. This is especially clear when the word is used in the same way of orders as of *ecclesiastical benefices*. These, by the undoubted teaching of the sacred canons, were clearly null if given with any vitiating defect. Moreover, when some doubted as to who, according to the mind of the Pontiff, could be called and considered Bishops *validly and lawfully ordained*, the said Pope shortly after, on October 30, issued further letters in the form of a Brief, and said: *We, wishing to remove the doubt, and to opportunely provide for the peace of conscience of those who, during the schism, were promoted to orders, by expressing more*

Apostolic Letter.

claratio, nisi apposite ad rem Angliae praesentem, id est ad Ordinale eduardianum, spectare debuisset, nihil certe confecerat Pontifex novis litteris, quo vel *haesitationem tolleret* vel *serenitati conscientiae consuleret.* Ceterum Apostolicae Sedis documenta et mandata non aliter quidem Legatus intellexit, atque ita eis rite religioseque obtemperavit : idque pariter factum a regina Maria et a ceteris qui cum ea dederunt operam ut religio et instituta catholica pristinum locum restituerentur.

Auctoritates quas excitavimus Iulii III. et Pauli IV. aperte ostendunt initia eius disciplinae quae tenore constanti, iam tribus amplius saeculis, custodita est, ut ordinationes ritu Eduardiano haberentur infectae et nullae; cui disciplinae amplissime suffragantur testimonia multa earumdem ordinationum quae,

clearly the mind and intention which we had in the aforesaid letters, declare that only those Bishops and Archbishops, who were not ordained and consecrated in the form of the Church, cannot be said to be validly and lawfully ordained. Unless this declaration had applied to the actual case in England—that is to say, to the Edwardine Ordinal— the Pope would certainly have done nothing by these last letters *for the removal of doubt, and the restoration of peace of conscience.* Further, it was in this sense that the Legate understood the documents and commands of the Apostolic See, and duly and conscientiously obeyed them; and the same was done by Queen Mary, and the rest who helped to restore the Catholic religion to its former state.

The authority of Julius III. and Paul IV., which we have quoted, clearly shows the origin of the practice, which has been observed without interruption for more than three centuries,

in hac etiam Urbe, saepius absoluteque iteratae sunt ritu catholico. In huius igitur disciplinae observantia vis inest opportuna proposito. Nam si cui forte quidquam dubitationis resideat in quamnam vere sententiam ea Pontificum diplomata sint accipienda, recte illud valet: *Consuetudo optima legum interpres.* Quoniam vero firmum semper ratumque in Ecclesia mansit, Ordinis sacramentum nefas esse iterari, fieri nullo pacto poterat ut talem consuetudinem Apostolica Sedes pateretur tacita ac toleraret. Atqui eam non toleravit solum, sed probavit etiam et sanxit ipsa, quotiescumque in eadem re peculiare aliquod factum incidit iudicandum. Duo eiusmodi facta in medium proferimus, ex multis quae ad *Supremam* sunt subinde delata: alterum, anno MDCLXXXIV., cuiusdam

that ordination according to the Edwardine rite should be considered null and void. This practice is fully proved by the numerous cases of absolute reordination according to the Catholic rite, even in Rome. In the observance of this practice we have a proof directly affecting the matter in hand, for if by any chance doubt should remain as to the true sense in which these Pontifical documents are to be understood, the principle holds good that *custom is the best interpreter of law.* Since in the Church it has ever been a constant and established rule that it is sacrilegious to repeat the Sacrament of Orders, it never could have come to pass that the Apostolic See should have silently acquiesced in and tolerated such a custom. But not only did the Apostolic See tolerate this practice, but approved and sanctioned it as often as any particular case arose which called for its judgment in the matter. We adduce two facts of this kind out of many which

Calvinistae Galli, alterum, anno MDCCIV., Ioannis Clementis Gordon; utriusque secundum rituale Eduardianum suos adepti ordines. In primo, post accuratam rei investigationem, consultores non pauci responsa sua, quae appellant vota, de scripto ediderunt, ceterique cum eis in unam conspirarunt sententiam, *pro invaliditate ordinationis:* tantum quidem ratione habita opportunitatis, placuit Cardinalibus respondere, *Dilata*. Eadem vero acta repetita et ponderata sunt in facto altero: quaesita sunt praeterea nova consultorum vota, rogatique doctores egregii e Sorbonicis ac Duacenis, neque praesidium ullum perspicacioris prudentiae praetermissum est ad rem penitus pernoscendam. Atque hoc animadvertisse oportet quod, tametsi tum ipse Gordon cuius negotium erat, tum aliqui consultores inter causas *nullitatis* vindicandae etiam adduxissent illam prout putabatur ordinationem Parkerii, in senten-

have from time to time been submitted to the Supreme Council of the Holy Office. The first was (in 1684) of a certain French Calvinist, and the other (1704) of John Clement Gordon, both of whom had received their Orders according to the Edwardine ritual. In the first case, after a searching investigation the consultors, not a few in number, gave in writing their answer, or, as they call it, their *vota*, and the rest unanimously agreed with their conclusion, *for the invalidity of the ordination*, and only on account of reasons of opportuneness did the Cardinals deem it well to answer by a *dilata* (viz., not to formulate the conclusion at the moment). The same documents were called into use and considered again in the examination of the second case, and additional written statements of opinion were also obtained from consultors, and the most eminent doctors of the Sorbonne and of the Douai Universities were likewise asked for their

tia tamen ferenda omnino seposita est ea causa, ut documenta produnt integrae fidei, neque alia ratio est reputata nisi *defectus formae et intentionis.* Qua de forma quo plenius esset certiusque iudicium, cautum fuerat ut exemplar Ordinalis anglicani suppeteret; atque etiam cum eo singulae collatae sunt formae ordinandi, ex variis orientalium et occidentalium ritibus conquisitae. Tum Clemens XI., Cardinalium ad quos pertinebat consentientibus suffragiis, ipsemet feria V., die XVII. aprilis MDCCIV., *decrevit:* "Ioannes Clemens Gordon *ex integro et absolute* ordinetur ad omnes ordines etiam sacros et praecipue presbyteratus, et quatenus non fuerit confirmatus, prius sacramentum Confirmationis suscipiat." Quae sententia, id sane considerare refert, ne a defectu quidem *traditionis instrumentorum* quidquam momenti duxit: tunc enim praescriptum de more esset ut ordinatio *sub conditione* instauraretur. Eo autem opinion. No safeguard which wisdom and prudence could suggest to ensure the thorough sifting of the question was neglected.

And here it is important to observe that although Gordon himself, whose case it was, and some of the consultors, had adduced, amongst the reasons which went to prove invalidity, the ordination of Parker, according to their own ideas about it, in the delivery of the decision this reason was altogether set aside, as documents of incontestable authenticity prove. In pronouncing the decision, weight was given to no other reason than the *defect of form and intention*, and, in order that the judgment concerning this form might be more certain and complete, precaution was taken that a copy of the Anglican Ordinal should be submitted to examination, and that with it should be collated the ordination forms gathered together from the various Eastern and Western rites.

Apostolic Letter.

pluris refert considerare, eamdem Pontificis sententiam spectare universe ad omnes Anglicanorum ordinationes. Licet enim factum attigerit peculiare, non tamen ex peculiari quapiam ratione profecta est, verum ex *vitio formae*, quo quidem vitio ordinationes illae aeque afficiuntur omnes: adeo ut, quoties deinceps in re simili decernendum fuit, toties idem Clementis XI. communicatum sit decretum.

Quae quum ita sint, non videt nemo controversiam temporibus nostris exsuscitatam, Apostolicae Sedis iudicio definitam multo antea fuisse: documentisque illis haud satis quam oportuerat cognitis, fortasse factum ut scriptor aliquis catholicus disputationem de ea libere habere non dubitarit. Quoniam vero, ut principio monuimus, nihil Nobis antiquius optatiusque est quam ut

Then Clement XI. himself, with the unanimous vote of the Cardinals concerned, on the *Feria V.*, April 17th, 1704, decreed: "John Clement Gordon shall be ordained *from the beginning and unconditionally*, to all the Orders, even sacred Orders, and chiefly of priesthood, and in case he has not been confirmed he shall first receive the sacrament of Confirmation." It is important to bear in mind that this judgment was in no wise determined by the omission of the rite of *handing over the instruments*, for in such a case, according to the established custom, the direction would have been to repeat the ordination *conditionally*. Still more important is it to note that the judgment of the Pontiff applies universally to all Anglican ordinations, because, although it refers to a particular case, it is not based upon any reason special to that case, but upon the *defect of form*, which defect equally affects all these ordinations,

hominibus recte animatis maxima possimus indulgentia et caritate prodesse, ideo iussimus in Ordinale anglicanum, quod caput est totius causae, rursus quam studiosissime inquiri.

In ritu cuiuslibet conficiendi et administrandi iure discernunt inter partem *caeremonialem* et partem *essentialem* quae *materia et forma* appellari consuevit. Omnesque norunt, sacramenta novae legis, utpote signa sensibilia atque gratiae invisibilis efficientia, debere gratiam et significare quam efficiunt et efficere quam significant. Quae significatio, etsi in toto ritu essentiali, in materia scilicet et forma, haberi debet, praecipue tamen ad formam pertinet; quum materia sit pars per se non determinata, quae per illam determinetur. Idque in sacramento Ordinis manifestius apparet cuius conferendi materia, qua-

so much so that when similar cases subsequently came up for decision the same decree of Clement XI. was quoted as the rule to follow.

Hence it must be clear to every one that the controversy, lately revived, had been already definitely settled by the Apostolic See, and that it is to the insufficient knowledge of these documents that we must, perhaps, attribute the fact that any Catholic writer should have considered it still an open question. But, as We stated at the beginning, there is nothing We so deeply and ardently desire as to be of help to men of good will by showing them the greatest consideration and charity, wherefore We ordered that the Anglican Ordinal, which is the essential point of the whole matter, should be at once most carefully examined.

In the examination of any rite for the effecting and administering of a sacrament, distinction is rightly made between the part

tenus hoc loco se dat considerandam, est manuum impositio; quae quidem nihil definitum per se significat, et aeque ad quosdam Ordines, aeque ad Confirmationem usurpatur. Iamvero verba quae ad proximam usque aetatem habentur passim ab Anglicanis tamquam forma propria ordinationis presbyteralis, videlicet, *Accipe Spiritum Sanctum*, minime sane significant definite ordinem sacerdotii vel eius gratiam et potestatem, quae praecipue est potestas *consecrandi et offerendi verum corpus et sanguinem Domini*[1], eo sacrificio, quod non est *nuda commemoratio sacrificii in Cruce peracti*.[2] Forma huiusmodi aucta quidem est postea iis verbis, *ad officium et opus presbyteri:* sed hoc potius con-

1 Trid. Sess. XXIII., *de. sacr. Ord. can. 1.*

2. *Ib.* Sess. XXII, *de sacrif. Missae, can.* 3.

which is *ceremonial* and that which is *essential*, usually called the "*matter and form.*" All know that the sacraments of the New Law, as sensible and efficient signs of invisible grace, ought both to signify the grace which they effect and effect the grace which they signify. Although the signification ought to be found in the whole essential rite, that is to say, in the matter and form, it still pertains chiefly to the form, since the matter is the part which is not determined by itself, but which is determined by the form; and this appears still more clearly in the Sacrament of Orders, the matter of which, in so far as we have to consider it in this case, is the imposition of hands, which indeed by itself signifies nothing definite, and is equally used for several orders, and for confirmation. But the words which, until recently, were commonly held by Anglicans to constitute the proper form of priestly ordination, namely: "*Receive the Holy Ghost*," cer-

vincit, Anglicanos vidisse ipsos primam eam formam fuisse mancam neque idoneam rei. Eadem vero adiectio, si forte quidem legitimam significationem apponere formae posset, serius est inducta, elapso iam saeculo post receptum Ordinale eduardianum; quum propterea, Hierarchiâ extincta, potestas ordinandi iam nulla esset. Nequidquam porro auxilium causae novissime arcessitum est ab aliis eiusdem Ordinalis precibus. Nam, ut cetera praetereantur quae eas demonstrent in ritu anglicano minus sufficientes proposito, unum hoc argumentum sit instar omnium, de ipsis consulto detractum esse quidquid in ritu catholico dignitatem et officia sacerdotii perspicue designat. Non ea igitur forma esse apta et sufficiens sacramento potest, quae id nempe reticet quod deberet proprium significare.

tainly do not in the least definitely express the sacred order of priesthood or its grace and power, which is chiefly the power *of consecrating and offering the true Body and Blood of the Lord* (Council of Trent, Sess. XXIII., *De Sacr. Ord.*, Can. 1.) in that sacrifice which is no "nude commemoration of the sacrifice offered on the cross." (Ibid. Sess. XXII., *De Sacrif. Missae*, Can. 3.) This form had indeed afterwards added to it the words, "*for the office and work of a priest,*" etc., but this rather shows that the Anglicans themselves perceived that the first form was defective and inadequate. But even if this addition could give to the form its due signification, it was introduced too late, as a century had already elapsed since the adoption of the Edwardine Ordinal; for as the Hierarchy had become extinct there remained no power of ordaining. In vain has help been recently sought for the plea of the validity of Orders from the other prayers of

De consecratione episcopali similiter est. Nam formulae, *Accipe Spiritum Sanctum*, non modo serius adnexa sunt verba, *ad officium et opus episcopi*, sed etiam de iisdem, ut mox dicemus, iudicandum aliter est quam in ritu catholico. Neque rei proficit quidquam advocasse praefationis precem, *Omnipotens Deus;* quum ea pariter deminuta sit verbis quae *summum sacerdotium* declarent. Sane, nihil huc attinet explorare, utrum episcopatus complementum sit sacerdotii, an ordo ab illo distinctus: aut collatus, ut aiunt, *per saltum*, scilicet homini non sacerdoti, utrum effectum habeat necne. At ipse procul dubio, ex institutione Christi, ad sacramentum Ordinis verissime pertinet, atque est praecellenti gradu sacerdotium; quod nimirum et voce sanctorum Patrum et rituali nostra consuetu-

the same Ordinal. For, to put aside other reasons which show this to be insufficient for the purpose in the Anglican rite, let this argument suffice for all, that from them has been deliberately removed whatever set forth the dignity and office of the priesthood in the Catholic rite. That form consequently ought not to be considered apt or sufficient for the sacrament which omits what it ought essentially to signify.

It is the same with regard to episcopal consecration. To the form " *Receive the Holy Ghost*" the words "*for the office and work of a Bishop*" were added at a later period; but even these words, as We shall presently show, must be understood in a sense different from that which they bear in the Catholic rite. Nor is there anything gained by quoting "*Almighty God,*" since it in like manner has been stripped of the words which denote the *High Priesthood*. It is not here relevant to examine whether the episcopate be

dine *summum sacerdotium, sacri ministerii summa* nuncupatur. Inde fit ut, quoniam sacramentum Ordinis verumque Christi sacerdotium a ritu anglicano penitus extrusum est, atque adeo in consecratione episcopali eiusdem ritus nullo modo sacerdotium confertur, nullo item modo episcopatus vere ac iure possit conferri: eoque id magis quia in primis episcopatus muniis illud scilicet est, ministros ordinandi in sanctam Eucharistiam et sacrificium.

Ad rectam vero plenamque Ordinalis anglicani aestimationem, praeter ista per aliquas eius partes notata, nihil profecto tam valet quam si probe aestimetur quibus adiunctis rerum conditum sit et publice constitutum. Longum est singula persequi, neque est necessarium: eius namque aetatis memoria satis diserte loquitur, cuius animi

a completion of the priesthood or an order distinct from it, or whether when bestowed as they say *per saltum* on one who is not a priest, it has or has not its effect. But the episcopate undoubtedly by the institution of Christ most truly belongs to the sacrament of Orders, and constitutes the priesthood in the highest degree—namely, that which by the teachings of the holy Fathers and our Liturgical customs is called the *Summum Sacerdotium, Sacri Ministerii Summa.*— ["The High Priesthood, the Fullness of the Sacred Ministry."] Thus we find that, as the Sacrament of Orders and the true priesthood of Christ were utterly eliminated from the Anglican rite, and hence the priesthood is in no wise conferred truly and validly in the episcopal consecration of the same rite, for the like reason, therefore, the episcopate can in no way be truly and validly conferred by it, and this the more so because among the duties of the episcopate

essent in Ecclesiam catholicam auctores Ordinalis, quos adsciverint fautores ab heterodoxis sectis, quo demum consilia sua referrent. Nimis enimvero scientes quae necessitudo inter fidem et cultum, inter *legem credendi et legem supplicandi* intercedat, liturgiae ordinem, specie quidem redintegrandae eius formae primaevae, ad errores Novatorum multis modis deformarunt. Quamobrem toto Ordinali non modo nulla est aperta mentio sacrificii, consecrationis, sacerdotii, potestatisque consecrandi et sacrificii offerendi; sed immo omnia huiusmodi rerum vestigia, quae superessent in precationibus ritus catholici non plane reiectis, sublata et deleta sunt de industria, quod supra attigimus. Ita per se apparet nativa Ordinalis indoles ac spiritus, uti l o q u u n t u r. Hinc vero ab origine ducto

is that of ordaining ministers for the Holy Eucharistic Sacrifice.

For the accurate and full understanding of the Anglican Ordinal, besides what we have noted as to some of its parts, it is worthy of note to consider carefully the circumstances under which it was composed and publicly authorized. It would be tedious to enter into details, nor is it necessary to do so, as the history of that time is sufficiently eloquent as to the animus of the authors of the Ordinal against the Catholic Church, as to the abettors whom they associated with themselves from the heterodox sects, and as to the end they had in view. Being fully aware of the necessary connection between faith and worship, between *the law of believing and the law of praying*, under a pretext of returning to the primitive form, they corrupted in many ways the liturgical order to suit the errors of the reformers. For this reason in the whole Ordinal not only is there no clear mention of the Sacrifice, of consecration to the priesthood and of the power of consecrating and offering sacrifices, but, as We have just stated,

vitio, si valere ad usum ordinationum minime potuit, nequaquam decursu aetatum, quum tale ipsum permanserit, futurum fuit ut valeret. Atque ii egerunt frustra qui inde a temporibus Caroli I. conati sunt admittere aliquid sacrificii et sacerdotii, nonnullá dein ad Ordinale facta accessione: frustraque similiter contendit pars ea Anglicanorum non ita magna, recentiore tempore coalita, quae arbitratur posse idem Ordinale ad sanam rectamque sententiam intelligi et deduci. Vana, inquimus, fuere et sunt huiusmodi conata: idque hac etiam de causa, quod, si qua quidem verba, in Ordinali anglicano ut nunc est, porrigant se in ambiguum, ea tamen sumere sensum eumdem nequeunt quem habent in ritu catholico. Nam semel novato ritu, ut vidimus, quo nempe negetur vel adulteretur sacramentum Ordinis,

every trace of these things, which had been in such prayers of the Catholic rite as they had not entirely rejected, was deliberately removed and struck out. In this way the native character, or spirit, as it is called, of the Ordinal clearly manifests itself. Hence if vitiated in its origin it was wholly insufficient to confer Orders. It was impossible that in the course of time it would become sufficient, since no change had taken place. In vain those who from the time of Charles I. have attempted to hold some kind of sacrifice or of priesthood have made some additions to the Ordinal. In vain also has been the contention of that small section of the Anglican body, formed in recent times, that the said Ordinal can be understood and interpreted in a sound and orthodox sense. Such efforts we affirm have been and are made in vain, and for this reason that any words in the Anglican ordinal, as it now is, which lend themselves to ambiguity, cannot be taken in the same sense as they possess in the Catholic rite. For once a new rite has been instituted in which, as we have seen, the Sacrament

et a quo quaevis notio repudiata sit consecrationis et sacrificii; iam minime constat formula, *Accipe Spiritum Sanctum*, qui Spiritus, cum gratia nimirum sacramenti, in animam infunditur; minimeque constant verba illa, *ad officium et opus presbyteri* vel *episcopi* ac similia, quae restant nomina sine re quam instituit Christus. Huius vim argumenti perspectam ipsi habent plerique Anglicani, observantiores Ordinalis interpretes; quam non dissimulanter eis obiiciunt qui nove ipsum interpretantes, Ordinibus inde collatis pretium virtutemque non suam spe vana affingunt. Eodem porro argumento vel uno illud etiam corruit, opinantium posse in legitimam Ordinis formam sufficere precationem, *Omnipotens Deus, bonorum omnium largitor*, quae sub initium est ritualis actionis; etiamsi forte haberi ea of Orders is adulterated or denied, and from which all idea of consecration and sacrifice has been rejected, the formula, *Receive the Holy Ghost*, no longer holds good, because the Spirit is infused into the soul with the grace of the Sacrament; and the words *for the office and work of a priest or bishop*, and the like, no longer hold good, but remain as words without the reality which Christ instituted. Several of the more shrewd Anglican interpreters of the Ordinal have perceived the force of this argument, and they openly urge it against those who take the Ordinal in a new sense, and vainly attach to the Orders conferred thereby a value and efficiency they do not possess. By this same argument is refuted the contention of those who think that the prayer "*Almighty God giver of all good things*," which is found at the beginning of the ritual action, might suffice as a legitimate form of Orders, even in the hypothesis that it might

posset tamquam sufficiens in ritu aliquo catholico quem Ecclesia probasset. Cum hoc igitur intimo *formae defectu* coniunctus est *defectus intentionis*, quam aeque necessario postulat, ut sit, sacramentum. De mente vel intentione, utpote quae per se quiddam est interius, Ecclesia non iudicat: at quatenus extra proditur, iudicare de ea debet. Iam vero quum quis ad sacramentum conficiendum et conferendum materiam formamque debitam serio ac rite abhibuit, eo ipso censetur id nimirum facere intendisse quod facit Ecclesia. Quo sane principio, innititur doctrina quae tenet esse vere sacramentum vel illud, quod ministerio hominis haeretici aut non baptizati, dummodo ritu catholico, conferatur. Contra, si ritus immutetur, eo manifesto consilio ut alius inducatur ab Ecclesia non receptus, utque id repellatur

be held to be sufficient in a Catholic rite approved by the Church. With this inherent *defect of form* is joined the *defect of intention*, which is usually essential to the Sacraments. The Church does not judge about the mind and intention in so far as it is something by its nature internal, but in so far as it is manifested externally she is bound to judge concerning it. When any one has rightly and seriously made use of due form and the matter requisite for effecting or conferring the Sacrament, he is considered by the very fact to do what the Church does. On this principle rests the doctrine that a Sacrament is truly conferred by the ministry of one who is a heretic or unbaptized provided the Catholic rite be employed. On the other hand, if the rite be changed with the manifest intention of introducing another rite not approved by the Church, and of rejecting what the Church does, and what by the institution of Christ belongs to the

quod facit Ecclesia et quod ex institutione Christi ad naturam attinet sacramenti, tunc palam est, non solum necessariam sacramento intentionem deesse, sed intentionem immo haberi sacramento adversam et repugnantem.

Isthaec omnia diu multumque reputavimus apud Nos et cum Venerabilibus Fratribus Nostris in *Suprema* iudicibus; quorum etiam Coetum singulariter coram Nobis advocare placuit feria V., die XVI. iulii proximi, in commemoratione Mariae D. N. Carmelitidis. Iique ad unum consensêre, propositam causam iam pridem ab Apostolica Sede plene fuisse et cognitam et iudicatam: eius autem denuo instituta actâque quaestione, emersisse illustrius quanta illa iustitiae sapientiaeque pondere totam rem absolvisset. Verumtamen optimum factu duxi-

nature of the Sacrament, then, it is clear that not only is the necessary intention wanting to the Sacrament, but that the intention is adverse to and destructive of the Sacrament.

All these matters have been long and carefully considered by Ourselves and by Our venerable brethren, the Judges of the Supreme Council, of whom it has pleased Us to call a special meeting on Thursday, the 16th day of July last, feast of the Solemnity of Our Lady of Mount Carmel. They, with one accord, agreed that the question laid before them had been adjudicated upon with full knowledge of the Apostolic See, and that this renewed discussion and examination of the issue had only served to bring out more clearly the wisdom and accuracy with which that decision had been made. Nevertheless, We deemed it well to postpone a decision, in order to afford time both to consider whether it would be fitting

mus supersedere sententiae, quo et melius perpenderemus conveniret ne expediretque eamdem rem auctoritate Nostra rursus declarari, et uberiorem divini luminis copiam supplices imploraremus. Tum considerantibus Nobis ut idem caput disciplinae, etsi iure iam definitum, a quibusdam revocatum sit in controversiam, quacumque demum causa sit revocatum; ex eoque pronum fore ut perniciosus error gignatur non paucis qui putent se ibi Ordinis sacramentum et fructus reperire ubi minime sunt, visum est in Domino sententiam Nostram edicere.

Itaque omnibus Pontificum Decessorum in hac ipsa causa decretis usquequaque assentientes, eaque plenissime confirmantes ac veluti renovantes auctoritate Nostra, motu proprio certia scientia; pronunciamus et declaramus, Ordina-

or expedient that We should make a fresh authoritative declaration upon the matter, and to humbly pray for a fuller measure of Divine guidance. Then, considering that this matter of practice, although already decided, had been by certain persons for whatever reasons recalled into discussion, and that thence it might follow that a pernicious error would be fostered in the minds of many, who might suppose that they possessed the Sacraments and effects of Orders where those are nowise to be found, it has seemed good to Us in the Lord to pronounce Our judgment.

Wherefore, strictly adhering in this matter to the decrees of the Pontiffs, Our predecessors, and confirming them more fully, and as it were, renewing them by Our authority, of Our own free will and from certain knowledge, We pronounce and declare that Ordinations carried out according to the Anglican rites, have been, and are

Apostolic Letter. 33

tiones ritu anglicano actas, irritas prorsus fuisse et esse, omninoque nullas.

Hoc restat, ut quo ingressi sumus *Pastoris magni* nomine et animo veritatem tam gravis rei certissimam commonstrare, eodem adhortemur eos qui Ordinum atque beneficia sincera voluntate optent ac requirant. Usque adhuc fortasse, virtutis christianæ intendentes ardorem, religiosius consulentes divinas litteras pias duplicantes preces, incerti tamen haeserunt et auxii ad vocem Christi iamdiu intime admonentis. Probe iam vident quo se bonus ille invitet ac velit. Ad unicum eius ovile si redeant, tum vero et quaesita beneficia assecuturi sunt et consequentia salutis praesidia, quorum administram fecit ipse Ecclesiam, quasi redemptionis suae custodem perpetuam et procuratricem in gentibus. Tum vero *haurient aquas in gaudio de fontibus*

absolutely null and utterly void. It remains for Us to say that even as We have entered upon the elucidation of this grave question in the name and in the love of the Great Shepherd, in the same we appeal to those who desire and seek with a sincere heart the possession of a hierarchy and of Orders. Perhaps, until now, aiming at the greater perfection of Christian virtue, and searching more devoutly the Divine Scriptures, and redoubling the fervor of their prayers, they have nevertheless hesitated in doubt and anxiety to follow the voice of Christ, which has so long interiorly admonished them. Now, they see clearly whither He in His goodness invited them, and wills them to come. In returning to His one only fold they will obtain the blessings which they seek, and the consequent helps to salvation of which He has made the Church the dispenser, and, as it were, the constant guardian and promoter of His Redemption

Salvatoris, sacramentis eius mirificis; unde fideles animae in amicitiam Dei, remissis vere peccatis, restituuntur, caelesti pane aluntur et roborantur, adiumentisque maximis affluunt ad vitae adeptionem aeternae. Quorum bonorum revera sitientes, utinam *Deus pacis, Deus totius consolationis* facit compotes atque expleat perbenignus. Hortationem vero Nostram et vota eos maiorem in modum spectare volumus, qui religionis ministri in communitatibus suis habentur. Homines ex ipso officio praecedentes doctrina et auctoritate, quibus profecto cordi est divina gloria et animarum salus, velint alacres vocanti Deo parere in primis et obsequi, praeclarumque de se edere exemplum. Singulari certe laetitia eos Ecclesia mater excipiet omnique complectetur bonitate et providentia, quippe quos per arduas among the nations. Then, indeed, "they shall draw waters in joy from the fountains of the Savior," His wondrous sacraments, whereby His faithful souls have their sins truly remitted and are restored to the friendship of God, are nourished and strengthened by the Heavenly Bread, and abound with the most powerful aids for their eternal salvation. May the God of peace, the God of all consolation, in His infinite tenderness enrich and fill with these blessings those who truly yearn for them. We wish to direct Our exhortation and Our desires in a special way to those who are ministers of religion in their respective communities. They are men who from their very office take precedence in learning and authority, and who have at heart the glory of God and the salvation of souls.

Let them be the first in joyfully submitting to the Divine call, and obey it and furnish a glorious example to others. Assuredly with

Apostolic Letter. 35

rerum difficultates virtus animi generosior ad sinum suum reduxerit. Ex hac vero virtute dici vix potest quae ipsos laus maneat in coetibus fratrum per catholicum orbem, quae aliquando spes et fiducia ante Christum iudicem, quae ab illo praemia in regno caelesti! Nos quidem, quantum omni ope licuerit, eorum cum Ecclesia reconciliationem fovere non desistemus; ex qua et singuli et ordines, id quod vehementer cupimus, multum capere possunt ad imitendum. Interea veritatis gratiaeque divinae patentem cursum ut secundare contendant fideliter, per viscera misericordiae Dei nostri rogamus omnes et obsecramus.

Praesentes vero litteras et quaecumque in ipsis habentur nullo unquam tempore de subreptionis aut obreptionis sive intentionis Nostrae vitio aliove quovis de-

an exceeding great joy their mother the Church will welcome them, and will cherish with all her love and care those whom the strength of their generous souls has amidst many trials and difficulties led back to her bosom. Nor could words express the recognition which this devoted courage will win for them from the assemblies of the brethren throughout the Catholic world, or what hope or confidence it will merit for them before Christ as their Judge, or what reward it will obtain from Him in the Heavenly Kingdom. And We Ourselves in every lawful way shall continue to promote their reconciliation with the Church in which individuals and masses, as we ardently desire, may find so much for their imitation. In the meantime, by the tender mercy of the Lord Our God, We ask and beseech all to strive faithfully to follow in the open path of Divine grace and truth.

We decree that these Letters and all things contained

fectu notari vel impugnari posse; sed semper validas et in suo robore fore et esse, atque ab omnibus cuiusvis gradus et praeeminentiae inviolabiliter in iudicio et extra observari debere decernimus; irritum quoque et inane si secus super his a quoquam, quavis auctoritate vel praetextu, scienter vel ignoranter contigerit attentari declarantes, contrariis non obstantibus quibuscumque.

Volumus autem ut harum litterarum exemplis, etiam impressis, manu tamen Notarii subscriptis et per constitutum in ecclesiastica dignitate virum sigillo munitis, eadem habeatur fides quae Nostrae voluntatis significationi his praesentibus ostensis haberetur.

Datum Romae apud Sanctum Petrum anno Incarnationis Dominicae millesimo octingentesimo nonagesimo sexto, idibus septembribus,

therein shall not be liable at any time to be impugned or objected to by reason of fault or any other defect whatsoever of subreption or obreption, or of Our intention, but are and shall be always valid and in force, and shall be inviolably observed both juridically and otherwise, by all of whatsoever degree and pre-eminence, declaring null and void anything which in these matters may happen to be contrariwise attempted, whether wittingly or unwittingly, by any person whatsoever, by whatsoever authority or pretext, all things to the contrary notwithstanding.

We will that there shall be given to copies of these Letters, even printed, provided that they be signed by a notary and sealed by a person constituted in ecclesiastical dignity, the same credence that would be given to the expression of Our will by the showing of these presents.

Given at Rome, at St. Peter's, in the year of the Incarnation of Our Lord, one thousand eight hundred

Apostolic Letter.

Pontificatus Nostri anno decimo nono.

† C *Card.* DE RVGGIERO.
† A *Card.* BIANCHI,
Pro-Datarius.

Visa. .

De Cvria I. DE AQVILA, *E Vicecomitibus.*

Loco ✠ *Plumbi*
Reg. in Secret. Brevium.

I. CVGNONI.

and ninety-six, on the Ides of September, in the nineteenth year of Our Pontificate.

† C. *Card.* DE RUGGIERO.
† A. *Card.* BIANCI,
Pro-Datarius.

(*Visa.*) J. DELLA, AQUILA,
[SEAL.] *Visconti.*

Registered in the Secretariate of Briefs.

J. CUGNONI.

COMMENTARY ON THE BULL "APOSTOLICAE CURAE"

DECLARING NULL AND VOID THE RITE OF ORDINATION USED IN THE ANGLICAN CHURCH.

I.—INTRODUCTORY.

PUBLIC OPINION IN ENGLAND REGARDING THE BULL.

On September 8, 1896, the Feast of the Nativity of the Blesed Virgin Mary, was published the Bull "*Apostolicae Curae*" in which our Holy Father, Leo XIII., "*motu proprio certa scientia*," pronounced and declared that "ordinations performed according to the Anglican rite have been and are altogether invalid and absolutely null : "*Pronuntiamus et declaramus ordinationes ritu anglicano factas, irritas prorsus fuisse et esse omninoque nullas.*"

As might have been expected, this solemn and final decision, dreaded by a few but desired by many, has excited much comment in England. On the side of English Catholics it has been received with unanimous applause, and with every expression of the sincerest satisfaction and gratitude. It has afforded much consolation to all, but more especially to those converts who of late years have abandoned Anglicanism, and returned to the full and perfect obedience of the Roman Pontiff, in the true and only fold of Christ.[1]

The false and painful position created for them by the recent polemics is henceforth at an end : the Bull of Leo XIII., while it fully justifies their past action, gives

[1] From the conversion of Cardinal Newman to our own days there have been over 500 converts from the ranks of the Anglican ministry.

Commentary on the Bull "Apostolicae Curae." 39

them renewed energy and spurs them on to other and greater undertakings in behalf of those among their compatriots who are still separated from the centre of Catholic unity. The London *Tablet*, the official organ of English Catholics, speaks as follows of the Pontifical Bull:

"In the face of this document of the Holy See, our first duty is to express our filial gratitude to the Vicar of Christ for the fatherly zeal wherewith he has vouchsafed to put an end to the weighty and important question of Anglican Orders; for the elaborate and minute carefulness with which he has studied it; for the charity and fairness he has displayed in the various phases of the controversy; and in fine for the truly Apostolic uprightness of intention and the wonderful clearness with which he has delivered his supreme and final judgment in the matter. We are sure that the gratitude to which we give expression will be shared not only by the Catholics of England and English-speaking countries, but also by those of the whole world."[1]

The Catholic Truth Congress at Hanley echoed the sentiments of the *Tablet*, and at its first meeting on September 28, presided over by H. E. Cardinal Vaughan, moved, amid universal acclamations, a vote of thanks to the Holy Father, founded on the same reasons.

Furthermore, the English press has for the most part received the Papal document with respect and cordiality, printing it at length and with comments and acknowledging frankly that no one who believes and accepts Catholic doctrine can fail to appreciate the justice of the Pope's decision.

THE VIEW WHICH ENGLISH PROTESTANTS TAKE OF THE BULL.

In the same sense speak the English Protestants of the Erastian school, who constitute by far the majority

[1] *Tablet*, Sept 26, 1896.

of the Anglican Church. For even they, while showing a certain indifference with respect to the Papal document, profess themselves pleased with its publication, and glad to find themselves at one with the Pope in defending a truth so firmly supported by history, namely, that it was always the declared and explicit intention of the English Reformers of the XVI. century to exclude the Catholic priesthood and Sacrifice from their Church, absolutely and entirely. For example, let us hear what the *Rock*,[1] the spokesman of their school, says upon the subject:

"The Pope has spoken on the question of the Anglican Ordinations with a promptness and determination which many did not expect . . . We are fully in accord with the Pope in this matter, and we can subscribe to almost all his arguments. It is precisely what we have always held, namely, that by the Reformation the heads of the Church of England deliberately and effectively separated from the Church of Rome, repudiated her teaching on the Priesthood and on the Episcopacy, and therefore in the ordination they never had any intention of conferring the *Priesthood*, since they considered *Sacerdotalism* an injury to the Priesthood of Christ, without foundation in the Scriptures, and repugnant to all the cardinal doctrines of the Gospel."

The Exeter *Western Times*,[2] after having in a remarkable article censured severely the novelties of certain Anglicans "who desire at all costs to ape the Church of Rome," observes that the Pope has said in his Bull just what he ought to have said, that he shows a perfect appreciation of the genius of the English Reformation, in virtue of whose principles there does not and cannot exist a *sacrificing* priesthood in the Anglican Church. The writer concludes with the following noteworthy words: "If any disastrous consequence is to follow

---

[1] Sept. 25, 1896. "*Poor Lord Halifax.*"
[2] September 26, 1896.

from the publication of the Pontifical Bull, the disaster will not be due to the Church of Rome, but to those who have departed from the principles of the Reformation."

The Anglicans of this school are for the most part altogether in good faith, albeit full of old-fashioned prejudices against the Pope and the Church of Rome. At all events it may be said to their praise that, in rejecting priesthood and sacrifice, they are consistent with the principles on which their Church is founded. For this same Church, in the Thirty-first of its *Articles*, professes and teaches its members to hold firmly that: "*the Sacrifices of Masses*, in the which it was commonly said, that *the priest did offer Christ* for the quick and the dead, to have remission of pain or guilt, *were blasphemous fables and dangerous deceits.*"[1]

[It may be in place to add here that this view has been decidedly confirmed by the vague and unsatisfactory document intended as a reply to the Bull by the Anglican Archbishops of Canterbury and York.

The Ven. Archdeacon Taylor, of Liverpool, writes about this reply in the *English Churchman* as follows:

"With all due respect for the eminent prelates who have sent it forth, I cannot but regard it as altogether unsatisfactory and unworthy of the occasion. Far better to have left the Bull unanswered altogether. . . .

"The lengthy document contains a great amount of theological and liturgical research, but simply omits altogether the real point at issue. It never grapples with the real question. That question is plainly stated in the words of the Papal Bull (p. 30), but it is passed over by proving what no one denies, that the Reformers

---

1 Cardwell (Annals, I, 241) bears witness to the fact that from the very beginning of the Anglican Church its Bishops obliged the clergy to teach the people that "*The Mass* is not a propitiatory sacrifice for the living and the dead"

intended to continue the three orders of bishops, priests, and deacons in the church. That is not the question; but whether they intended that the priest should discharge precisely the same functions as before. The argument of the Bull is simple, intelligible, and on the premises laid down, conclusive, . . . and we owe him (the Pope) a debt of gratitude for so clearly proving the thoroughly Protestant character of our Church."

Other English as well as American papers of a representative character have taken the same view.—Ed.]

THE RITUALISTS.

Yet not all Anglicans—fortunately or unfortunately, it is hard to say,—belong to this school. For in fact there are some among them who are neither Protestants like their brethren, nor Catholics like us. An English Prelate has well defined them as *Protestants in Catholic disguise*. These originated in England about sixty years ago, in the so-called *Oxford* or *Tractarian Movement*, and are known to-day under the name of *Ritualists*. They profess, after a fashion, to believe in the priesthood, in the Sacrifice of the Mass, and in the Real Presence of Jesus Christ in the Eucharist. We say "after a fashion," for they do not understand these dogmas in the same sense in which the Catholic Church understands, and always has understood them. They recognize in the Mass only a commemorative sacrifice; and although they teach the presence of Christ in the Eucharist, yet they explain it in a Lutheran sense, or as an indefinable spiritual presence. They all, however, reject the Catholic doctrines of Transubstantiation; of the Constitution of the Church; of the Roman Pontiff's primacy of jurisdiction, and many others. Nevertheless, they hold that the supernatural life of the soul is created, nurtured and perfected by the Sacraments; and that the priests who

Commentary on the Bull "Apostolicae Curae." 43

administer them have power to consecrate, to sacrifice, and to absolve from sin. Since such a power essentially depends on the valid succession of the Catholic priesthood, it is plain why Ritualists have always been anxious to assure themselves as to the validity of the orders received in the Anglican Church. To this end they have sought more than once, but always in vain, some kind of recognition of their Orders from the Greeks, from the Dutch Jansenists; lately, from the "Old Catholics" of Germany; but all their endeavors have been in vain. On the other hand, many of their own people have been filled with serious doubts, as is attested by the striking fact that Dr. F. G. Lee— whc himself wrote what was for long considered the best defence of Anglican Orders—actually solicited, at the hands of some schismatical Bishops, who make use of a rite acknowledged by the Catholic Church, all the orders, inclusive of the episcopate, so that he and those who applied for the same favor with him might, in time, administer them to others; and it is understood that they in turn have ordained, by the same rite, a considerable number of applicants from among the Anglican clergy. Under such circumstances, which were somewhat discouraging, it was determined at last to approach the Holy See with the plea (suggested by Lord Halifax, the leader of a faction belonging to a not very large party of the Ritualists) that if the Roman Pontiff would recognize—were it only conditionally—the validity of these Orders, the way might be smoothed to a possible corporate reunion of the Church of England with that of Rome.

Disappointed.

To this party the solemn and final condemnation pronounced by Leo XIII. could not be otherwise than grievously displeasing. With one rude blow the Pope

dispelled their fond dream that the "Roman Branch" of the Catholic Church could recognize the Orders of the "Anglican Branch" as of equal value and efficacy with its own. It was but natural that together with this dream should also vanish that favorite Branch-theory, according to which the Church was to be *one*, not by unity of faith and government, as Leo XIII. teaches in his Encyclical *Satis Cognitum*, but simply by the unity or sameness of the sacraments, which are claimed by the diverse and independent "Branches" or national Churches, into which it is divided. Their disappointment has been all the more bitter because great hopes of a different solution had been pictured for them during the last two years, not only by the leaders of the *English Church Union*, but also through the not wholly discreet zeal of certain Catholic writers.[1]

All this may explain the irritation and pretended disdain which their periodicals affect now that the decision has been made plain by the publication of the Bull, but it can surely not excuse, or much less justify, the offensive innuendos and slanderous accusations with which some of them have sought to discredit the Pontifical Document.

To all these charges and insinuations we shall make fitting answer in the course of this inquiry; but, first of all, let us repeat here to our separated brethren the assurance given by H. E. Cardinal Vaughan in his speech at Hanley, that nothing short of irrefutable evidence, urgent charity, and imperative duty could have induced Leo XIII. to pronounce a final judgment on the invalid-

---

1. See e. g. the *Guardian* in its issues of September 23 and 30, of 1896. This is one of those journals which in the early months of 1896, echoing the sentiments of Messrs. Lacey, Puller and other ritualists and favorers of ritualism well known at Rome, were loud in praising the wisdom, impartiality, broad-mindedness, etc., of the Holy Father.

ity of their Orders. Set by God to govern His Church upon earth, he is her supreme Head, her infallible teacher, the chief guardian of her sacraments, her only safe guide through the often uncertain paths of truth and right. A debtor to God and souls alike, in the fulfillment of this his office, it would have been cruel not to dissipate that most baneful error which envelopes so many of his children, who, whilst still separated from him, are sincerely seeking the Kingdom of Christ in the unity of faith. There can be no doubt that Leo XIII., as in every other case, so especially in the present one, is moved solely by the Apostolic solicitude and love "in which," as he says in the beginning of the Bull, "aided by His grace, We strive according to Our ability to imitate and resemble the great Pastor of the sheep, Our Lord Jesus Christ."

HISTORIC ORIGIN OF THE ANGLICAN DIFFICULTY.

Henry VIII. was the English King who first forced the clergy and people of a Church, till then justly proud of the title of "*nobilissimum Sedis Apostolicae membrum*,"[1] to separate from the See of Peter. Having in 1534 rebelled against Clement VII., because that Pope could not allow him a divorce from his lawful wife, Henry VIII. proclaimed himself Head of the Church in England, and compelled his subjects to swear adhesion to this new dogma.[2] Thus began the Anglican schism, and religious anarchy in England. To a mere layman, named Cromwell, was committed the ecclesiastical government, as Vicar General of the Crown in spiritual things; the principal sees were filled with bishops notorious for their heresy and rabid Protestantism, whilst the preachers of the Reformation were allowed to wander everywhere unmolested in the propagation of their heresy. For the rest, although it is undeniable, as two Anglican ministers have recently acknowledged at Rome,[3] that under the schismatic Henry who died Janu-

1. Epist. Greg. IX. ad Suffraganeos Eccles. Cantuar.
2. Act of Supremacy, 26, Henry VIII, cc. 1, 2, 3.
3. Messrs. Lacey and Puller, *De Re Anglicana*. We allude to Messrs. Lacey and Puller, who, having labored strenuously to enlighten the *Curia* on the question of Anglican Orders, issued last May (1896) a work entitled *De Re Anglicana*, which they published secretly at Rome, and distributed broadcast among the Cardinals and Roman prelates. A translation of these two documents—Mr. Lacey's *De Re Anglicana*, and the *Risposta* of Dom Gasquet and Canon Moyes—was published in the *Tablet*. (Nov. 7th, 14th and 27th, 1896.) The immediate object of this publication was to correct a false impression as to the nature of the *Risposta*, to which the *Guardian* and the *Church Times* had previously given currency. These papers, whilst they published selections from the *Risposta*, suppressed all mention of its true character as a criticism on the *De Re Anglicana*, and gave the impression that it set forth the sole reasons, which had determined the English commissioners to petition for the condemnation of Anglican Orders:—in other words, these papers suggested that

Commentary on the Bull "Apostolicae Curae." 47

ary 28, 1547, there happened "quaedam (multa?) facinorosa, quaedam adhuc ploranda,"[1] nevertheless it is certain that during this first period of the Anglican schism (1534-1547) the Catholic Liturgy was maintained intact, and the *forma Ecclesiae consueta*, the customary form of the Church was used in Holy Ordinations. As to the validity of these Orders there is no doubt, nor does the recent Bull of Leo XIII. refer to them in any way.

CRANMER AND THE ANGLICAN ORDINAL.

But Thomas Cranmer, the unworthy Archbishop of Canterbury, chosen by Henry to be his instrument in bringing about the complete schism, was anxious to abolish the Catholic Liturgy in England and to fashion the ritual and religious practices after the pattern of the German Protestant sects. For this purpose he kept up a regular and close correspondence with the founders of these sects. With the death of Henry his longed-for opportunity arrived. Finding himself appointed, by the will of the late monarch, to the second place in the Council of the Regency of Edward VI. (who had succeeded his father at the age of about nine years), Cranmer made haste to carry his sinister designs into execution. Amongst the more important novelties which he caused to be approved by Parliament the chief were the suppression[2] of the Missal in favor of the

---

the *Risposta* convicted the Commission and the Roman authorities of having decided the merits of a theological and historical question solely on grounds of political expediency. What added to the strange character of this episode is the fact that Messrs. Lacey and Puller who, as authors of the *De Re Anglicana*, could not be ignorant of the facts, in no wise deemed it their duty to protest against this false imputation on the personal honor of their opponents.

1. Opusc. cit.

2. The Missal was suppressed by Act of Parliament, January 15, 1549. The *Ordinal*, as a substitute for the Pontifical, was approved

Protestant *communion office*, and the institution of a *new* rite called the *Ordinal*, which was to be followed in ordinations in place of the ancient Catholic *Pontifical* used for so many centuries in the Church of England.

We have called this *Ordinal* a *new* rite (and it is so called in the Bull, "*Novus plane ritus*,") for in reality the compilers of the *Ordinal*, in abandoning the rite of the Roman Pontifical would not and could not accept any of the ancient rites recognized as valid by the Catholic Church. The reason of this fact is evident from the scope they had in view, which was to exclude from the Anglican liturgy all *sacerdotalism*, and every trace of the Catholic doctrine about the Real Presence and the Eucharistic Sacrifice. Now, if the rite prescribed by the Pontifical was deliberately rejected, precisely because it was crammed full of formulas and ceremonies which asserted, supposed and signified the priesthood, the Real Presence, and the Sacrifice, how could they accept the rites, say, of the Greeks, or Maronites, or

a year after, in 1550. The final revision of the new liturgy was carried out in 1552. There is a disposition among Anglican controversialists to speak as though before the Reformation a variety of ordination rites existed in England, and to infer from the fact of such a variety that local churches had always enjoyed the right to draw up such services for themselves; a right, therefore, which the Reforming prelates were as much entitled to use as their predecessors. In view of this tendency among controversalists it is well to remember that the different pre-Reformation Pontificals—the Sarum, the Exeter, the Winchester, etc., were not different rites but the same rite, with merely a few slight variations of text and ceremony in purely minor matters. The proportion of these local variations to the portion which is identical in them all is not more than one to a hundred, if as much. And what is said of the ancient English Pontificals can be similarly said of all the Pontificals of the West. They are all the one and the same text, with merely a very few unimportant variants of phraseology and ceremony. Hence what Cranmer did was to lay sacrilegious hands on a rite which had been in use throughout the entire Western Church from time immemorial.

Commentary on the Bull "Apostolicae Curae." 49

Nestorians, or Jacobites of Alexandria, or Armenians, or of others which are governed by these same conceptions no less than the Roman rite, ancient and modern?[1]

Let us observe some of the characteristic notes of the *Anglican Ordinal* for the conferring of those three orders which it in some sense recognizes—diaconate, priesthood, episcopate. In the *Ordinal*, as we have already noticed, there is not a word which hints at a priestly power of consecrating, and offering in sacrifice to God the Body and Blood of Jesus Christ, really present under the species of bread and wine; the consecration of the candidate with holy oils is left out; also all the ceremonies with their accompanying forms used by the Church to signify the said powers, such as the delivery of the instruments, for example, the chalice and paten with host in the case of the priesthood. Even that most ancient eucharistic prayer, called the *consecratory* prayer, which is common to all rites, is not only changed and adulterated in this *Ordinal*, but furthermore is separated from the laying-on of hands, and is recited just like any other preparatory prayer. Moreover, not one of the *new forms* used in the *Ordinal*[2] expresses the power, or the order, which is to be conferred. How much of this *Ordinal*, known as the *Ordinal of Edward VI.*, came from the pen of Cranmer himself it is not easy to determine; but it is beyond dispute that he directed its composition, that he introduced into it the *new forms*, and that together with his

---

1. The text of these rites can be seen in Assemani's *Codex Liturgicus Eccl. Univ.* Tomi viii., ix., xi.; in his *Bibliotheca Orientalis*, Tom. iii.; also in Morinus, *De Sacris Ecclesiae Ordinationibus;* Denzinger, *Ritus Orientalium;* Duchesne, *Origines du Culte Chrétien;* Maskell, *Monumenta Ritualia, etc., etc.*

2 That is, in the Ordinal as it issued from the hands of its first compilers and was in use during the first century of Anglicanism. The additions made in 1662 will be referred to presently.

colleagues he willed that it should be substituted for the *Pontifical* with the open, deliberate and heretical intention of excluding the Catholic Priesthood and Sacrifice from the Church of England.

In speaking of Anglican Orders we speak always, and only, of those Orders which were (and are) conferred with the aforesaid Ordinal. So, also, it is only of these Orders that the Bull speaks when it says: "Ordinationes *ritu anglicano* actas irritas prorsus fuisse et esse, omninoque nullas."

Another fact which it is well to mention here, and to which we shall refer more than once in the following paragraphs, is that during the short reign of Edward VI. (1547-1553), the episcopal consecrations of Poynet, Hooper, Coverdale, Scory, Taylor and Harley were performed in England in conformity with the new *Ordinal*. This fact, which some have tried to deny, is fully certified by history. The authentic documents and manuscripts which prove it are referred to by Burnet, Fox, Estcourt and other English writers of equal weight.

The Ordinal under Mary and Elizabeth.

On the death of Edward, July 6, 1553, his legitimate sister, Mary, was proclaimed Queen of England. She had always remained Catholic and attached to the Apostolic See of Rome. On her ascent to the throne, and as long as she lived, she labored earnestly to repair the religious ruins caused by her father and brother, and to recall England to her ancient communion with the Church of Rome. In this work she had the effective and intelligent co-operation of Cardinal Pole who had been sent to her expressly by Pope Julius III., in the capacity of Papal Legate, with the fullest necessary faculties. One of the first acts of the reign of Mary was to remove, by the Legate's authority, the six "bishops"

aforesaid from the sees which they occupied, and to abrogate the new Liturgy, together with the Edwardine *Ordinal*, restoring in its full vigor the old Catholic *Pontifical* to be used in all ordinations.

It is to the first three years of Mary's reign that the four most important documents, quoted by Leo XIII. in his Bull belong. Of these, two are of Julius III., two of Paul IV., and they bear respectively the dates August 5, 1553, March 8, 1554, June 20, and October 30, 1555. From the whole four, as we shall presently see, it is clear that the question of the validity of Anglican Orders had already been seriously studied and decided by the Holy See not only under its practical but under its doctrinal aspect.

But unfortunately the reign of Mary was even shorter than that of her brother Edward; and she died in the November of 1558, having reigned four years and four months.

To her succeeded Elizabeth, the daughter of Henry VIII. and his notorious mistress Ann Boleyn. It is to Elizabeth that we owe the return of the evil days of heresy and schism upon England, which thenceforth never ceased. In the February of 1559, scarce three months after the death of her sister, by an Act of Parliament called together by her for the purpose, she suppressed once more the Roman Pontifical, and restored the use of the Liturgy and *Ordinal* of Edward VI.

The Catholic bishops legitimately nominated and consecrated under the reign of Mary were then required to apostatise, and to take that same iniquitous oath which had been enjoined by Henry and by Edward; they were to separate themselves from the centre of Catholic unity established by Christ in the Church of Rome, to deny the jurisdiction of the Holy See and to acknowledge Elizabeth as "supreme governor" of the Church in England. However, if one has to regret the cowar-

dice of so many bishops who bent before the tyranny of Henry, it is consoling to learn that among the Catholic bishops, living at Elizabeth's accession to the throne, there was but one Judas, whilst the rest faced courageously the loss of their sees, incarceration, and various other persecutions.[1]

Modification Introduced in the Rite.

But now Elizabeth's difficulties began. Desirous to see her Church founded on *aristocratic* principles she saved from the general destruction the three hierarchical Orders, although counting it of no great consequence whether or not her ministers were endowed with the sacramental character. With such thought in her mind she herself nominated the candidates whom she wished to intrude into the sees vacated by their lawful pastors. Amongst these candidates Matthew Parker, formerly chaplain to Ann Boleyn, was designated to the See of Canterbury. But how was he to be consecrated? All the Catholic bishops refused their services, not excepting Bishop Kitchen, he who alone had submitted to the sacrilegious oath. In such perplexity, after a short delay, Elizabeth issued her mandate of consecration, which was accepted by Coverdale and by his three

---

[1] In the *Registrum diversarum scripturarum Angliae, Scotiae, Hiberniae*, etc., preserved in the secret Archives of the Vatican, there is to be found a letter written to Cardinal Morone which is referred to this period. There we read: "In England there are at present 27 Cathedral Churches whereof 15 are vacant through the death of the Catholic bishops who had been put in possession legitimately by the Apostolic See. The bishops of the other 12 are still alive; and of these ten are prisoners in the Tower simply for the Catholic faith, and the authority of the Apostolic See which they are resolved to obey, and to suffer any torment ere they will acknowledge any other Head of God's Church than the Pope. Of the two other living bishops, he of S. Asaph is at the Council of Trent by order of your Holiness, while the Bishop of Llandaff has allowed himself to be seduced into obeying the Queen."—Cf. W. Maziere Brady, *Annals of the Catholic Hierarchy*, Rome, 1877, p. 4.

brother apostates, Barlow, Scory and Hodgkins. Barlow had been nominated by Henry VIII. to the Bishopric of St. David's in 1536, *i. e.*, at the beginning of the schism. It is, however, uncertain whether he ever received episcopal consecration, as all positive proof of the fact is lacking.[1]

Scory and Coverdale, as we saw above (page 50), had been consecrated according to the Edwardine *Ordinal*. As to Hodgkins there is no doubt but that he was consecrated bishop under Henry VIII., according to the Catholic Pontifical. These, therefore, were the consecrators of Parker; and if we are to trust the Act which is preserved in Parker's Archiepiscopal Register at Lambeth Palace, we must hold it for an historical fact that on Dec. 17, 1559, Parker was consecrated according to the Edwardine *Ordinal* by Barlow, assisted by the three prelates just mentioned, who were associated with him not merely in laying-on hands, but also in pronouncing the words of the Anglican form: *Take the Holy Ghost, and remember that thou stir up the grace of God which is in thee by the imposition of hands; for God hath not given us the spirit of fear, but of power, and love and soberness.*

Being himself consecrated after this fashion, Archbishop Parker in his turn consecrated the other candi-

[1] Mgr. Gasparri in his work *De la valeur des Ordinations Anglicanes* (Paris, 1895, p. 22), holds the consecration of Barlow to be historically certain and assures us that, after reading the Apologetic Dissertation *De Hierarchia Anglicana* published, by Messrs. Lacey and Denny, *aucun doute n'est resté dans mon esprit*. We, too, have read the said Dissertation but we confess after having also read what has been written on this point by Estcourt (*The Question of Anglican Orders Discussed*, London, 1873), by Fr. Sydney Smith, (*Reasons for Rejecting Anglican Orders*. Catholic Truth Society, London, 1895), and recently by the *Tablet*, we have been greatly confirmed in our doubts. But to our present purpose this point is of little or no importance, since the final condemnation of Anglican Orders in no way depends on that controversy.

dates nominated by Elizabeth, and these their successors, and so on, all following the new *Ordinal* which from that day to this has, with the exception of one modification, been constantly and faithfully followed in all the ordinations of the English Church.

The modification referred to consists in the addition of some words to the Edwardine form signifying the particular power to be conferred. Thus in the form of Episcopal consecration, to the words "*Take the Holy Ghost*" are added "*for the office and work of a bishop in the Church of God.*" But such a change not being introduced till a hundred and three years after the consecration of Parker—when, if the original Edwardine form was invalid, there was no longer a single validly consecrated Anglican bishop in the country—cannot affect this controversy, except perhaps by indicating that the Anglicans themselves were, at the latter time, convinced of the defectiveness of the form they had been using for more than a century. In other words—as the Holy Father has most wisely observed in the Bull—"Eadem adjectio, si forte quidem legitimam significationem apponere formae posset, serius est inducta, elapso iam saeculo post receptum Ordinale Eduardianum; quum propterea, Hierarchia extincta, potestas ordinandi iam nulla esset."

The Story of the "Nag's Head."

Before concluding this brief historical sketch, which, though not absolutely necessary, aids us in the full understanding and defence of the Pontifical document, it will not be out of place to touch on another point, therein alluded to, which relates to this same consecration of Parker.

According to an old story, at the beginning of Elizabeth's reign her candidates for the episcopate were supposed to have assembled at a tavern in London called

the *Nag's Head*, where their consecration was performed in the following way. While Parker and the other candidates knelt, Bishop Scory laid an open Bible on the head of each, saying: "Receive authority to preach the pure word of God." Then taking Parker by the hand he said: "Arise, Bishop of Canterbury!" This story, though it gained credence for a time, must unquestionably be rejected as untrue—at least in the sense of containing the denial of the Lambeth consecration. The evidence now in hand places it beyond doubt that Archbishop Parker did undergo a ceremony of consecration at Lambeth on Dec. 17, 1559; nor can the accounts recorded in the Lambeth register be far from the truth. There must, however, have been some feature in the Lambeth ceremony, which caused anxiety to the perpetrators, for they evidently desired to conceal its celebration from the Catholics. This is proved by the controversy between Harding and Jewell (see *Dublin Review*, Jan. 1896), in which Harding tries his best to elicit from his adversary what the facts were, but cannot succeed. Such being the policy of reserve adopted in regard to an event which the Government might have been expected to proclaim even on the house-tops, it was not wonderful that the Catholics should have speculated among themselves, and have given too easy a credence to a legendary account.[1] It ought not, how-

---

[1] One cannot be held responsible for what may be written on this or any other subject by incompetent writers, but for a long time past no English Catholic writer of any standing has used the Nag's Head story as an argument. If on the Continent two exceptions to this rule can be cited—Mgr. Gasparri (*De Sacra Ordinatione*, n. 4) and Perrone (*De Ordine*, n. 137, nota 4),—this must be ascribed to their comparative unfamiliarity with the English Catholic literature on the subject. Mgr. Gasparri, however, retracted his former teaching in his later work. (*De la valeur des Ordinations Anglicanes*), and Fr. Perrone, though he gives the story in a footnote, as a piece of crudition, expressly states that it was rejected by Dr. Lingard.

ever, to be forgotten that from the time of Champneys (1618), the corypheus among the early writers against Anglican Orders, other reasons besides the Nag's Head Story, and, chief among them, the reasons on which the Bull insists, have always been alleged and discussed.

What has been the genuine and authoritative "Roman teaching" from the very first beginnings of this controversy, we shall have occasion to explain in the course of this work. Let it suffice for the present to assert, on the faith of valuable documents before us, that the so-called "Nag's Head Story" was known and discredited at Rome as early as 1684-85, when for the first time the question of Anglican Orders was submitted to the authoritative judgment of the Congregation of the Holy Office at Rome.[1] We shall see, too, that the reason drawn from the absence of a proper form and intention (*defectus formae et intentionis*), on which Leo XIII. based his final judgment adverse to the validity of these Orders, has been likewise the *sole* reason which in every case determined the decisions of his predecessors and of the aforesaid Congregation in this matter. Whence it will be clear how truly their Eminences, the judges of the S. Congregation, in a special meeting *coram Sanctissimo*, on Thursday, July 16th, 1896, could assert that—as we read in the Bull: "The question laid before them had been already adjudicated upon with the full knowledge of the Apostolic See, and that this renewed discussion and examination of the issues had only served to bring out more clearly the wisdom and accuracy with which that decision had been made."

---

[1] In the authentic Acts of that time it is said expressly that the concordant judgment of the consulting theologians against the validity of the said Orders was given without making any account of the doubt relative to the *fact* of Parker's ordination, which was founded on historical "*testimonia sat confusa et perplexa.*"

PART II.

THE JUDGMENT OF LEO XIII.

Reasons which Prompted the Pontiff to Decide Against the Validity of Anglican Orders.

The decisive reason upon which Leo XIII. founds his final decision against the validity of Anglican Orders is that *absence of a proper form and intention* which has vitiated them all from 1550, when the Edwardine *Ordinal* was substituted for the Catholic Pontifical, down to the present time in which the same *Ordinal* (with the change already mentioned) continues to be the rite used.

From his Bull it is evident that the Holy Father has reached this conclusion not only after having ascertained the mind of his predecessors and the practice of the Holy See with regard to the same Orders, but also, and more especially, after a long and careful study of the Ordinal itself, considered both in itself and in the light of those historical circumstances which illustrate its real meaning, and determine the true and only end for which it was created and substituted for the ancient rites. This new investigation was made, as it ought to have been, without rejecting any of the numerous means wherein modern criticism abounds. "It has, therefore, pleased us graciously," writes the Pope, "to permit the cause to be re-examined, so that through the extreme care taken

in the new examination, all doubt, or even shadow of doubt, should be removed for the future."

This we wish to emphasise, even before giving more particular proofs of it, so as to make manifest the rashness of Ritualists like Mr. Lacy [1] and others, who, eager at all costs to throw discredit on the Pontifical document, are not ashamed to assert that Leo XIII. has defined against their Orders, not from a study of their intrinsic merits, but only lest by approving them he should seem to contradict his predecessors. Surely it is inconceivable that with the text of the Bull under their eyes they should permit themselves to bring such charges, for the Bull asserts in express terms that the Pope did order a fresh and independent investigation, and it devotes six pages to set forth the lines which the fresh investigation followed and the result it reached.

JULIUS III. AND THE EARLY ORDINATIONS ACCORDING TO THE ORDINAL OF EDWARD VI.

Following in the course of our inquiry the order observed by the Holy Father, we shall first of all examine what was the judgment of the Holy See in regard to the first ordinations, performed according to the new rite during the last three years of the reign of Edward VI., *i. e.*, from the first appearance of the *Ordinal*, in 1550, till the death of that monarch in 1553, when Queen Mary abrogated the new Anglican Liturgy and restored the use of the ancient Catholic Pontifical at all ordinations. This judgment of the Holy See is found clearly expressed in the four Apostolic Letters of Popes Julius III. and Paul IV., already referred to.

Julius III., desirous, with the Queen's help, to recall England to the bosom of the Catholic Church, sent to

---

[1] See the *Contemporary Review* (Dec., 1896,) and the *Guardian* (Dec. 9th, 1896.)

her Cardinal Pole to whom, as his Legate, he entrusted the fullest requisite faculties.[1] Now, amongst these faculties there was expressly that of *rehabilitating*, or of simply *habilitating*, to the exercise of the sacred ministry those ecclesiastics who had been exercising it under Kings Henry VIII. and Edward VI. The *rehabilitation* was to be used in favor of those only who, "*ante eorum lapsum in haeresim huiusmodi, rite et legitime promoti vel ordinati fuissent.*"[2] The simple *habilitation* referred to those who had not been "*rite et legitime promoti ad sacros ordines,*" that is, as the same Pontiff explains it in his Brief of March 8, 1554, those who had been ordained "*non servata forma Ecclesiae consueta.*" These, *si digni et idonei reperti fuissent* (if found fit), should, in order to be able to serve in the sanctuary, be promoted to all the sacred Orders up to priesthood by their Ordinaries; *ad omnes etiam sacros et presbyteratus ordines ab eorum ordinariis promoveri.*

And now who were these, ordained indeed, yet not ordained *servata forma Ecclesiae consueta?* When we reflect that in those three years (1550-1553), as Leo XIII. points out in his Bull,[3] and as we ourselves have just

1 See for text: *Bulla diei 5ae. augusti 1553, quae vocatur institutoria Card. Poli, Legati.* (Arch. Secr. Vatic., Cf. *Documenta ad Legationem Poli spectantia,* Roma, 1896, pp. 3-7; also Wilkins *Concilia* (IV. p. 91), and Burnet's *Collection of Records.* (P. III, Bk. V. n. 17.)

2 "Before their fall into heresy had been duly and lawfully promoted and ordained." Such were all those who had been ordained, before the new *Ordinal* had been substituted for the Catholic Pontifical.

3 "Besides it (the Edwardine form) and the Catholic form there was no other at that time in England." This statement has been challenged on the ground that Edward VI. permitted John A. Lasco and his German congregation to appoint their own ministers by their own rite; but to suggest that Julius III. may have had this German rite in view is to have recourse to what can only be called a miserable subterfuge. Besides which, even if it were necessary to take this into account, the Bull of Julius III. uses a negative phrase which excludes all forms whatever save the "accustomed form of the Church."

seen, there was no other form of ordination existing in
England except the *new* one which Edward VI. substituted for the *forma Ecclesiae consueta*, it is evident that
the persons alluded to were, and must have been, those
who were ordained with that *Ordinal*. If therefore
these men were, according to the express command of
Julius III., to be considered as simply laymen, and were
not to be admitted to the sacred ministry until they had
been re-ordained *absolutely* and without qualification,
according to the Catholic form, we are compelled to
conclude, that the ordinations which they received by
means of the Anglican *Ordinal* were judged by that
Pope, in 1553-4, not otherwise than they have been
judged in 1896 by Leo XIII., *i. e.*, *irritas prorsus omninoque nullas*.

PAUL IV. EXAMINES AND DECIDES THE QUESTION IN 1555.

Nor was the judgment any different which Paul IV.
pronounced upon the same Orders when, in 1555, he
succeeded Julius III., after the twenty-one days' Pontificate of Marcellus II. Before retailing the words of Paul
IV., Leo XIII. in his Bull recalls the fact that a solemn
embassy was sent to Rome, February 1555, by Queen
Mary and her consort King Philip. The point of this
reminder can escape nobody who understands the inti-
mate connection of cause and effect, of question and
answer which exists between the said embassy and the
Apostolic Letter of Paul IV., dated June 20, 1555. From
the documents in reference to it, which are kept in the
Vatican Archives,[1] we learn that its purpose was to
obtain from the Roman Pontiff a complete reconcilia-

---

[1] *Della Riduttione del Regno d'Inghilterra, Sommario primo*
(Arch. Vat. Arm. 64, Tom. 28, fol. 144); *Summarium eorum quae
confirmari petuntur a Sede Apostolica pro Anglis*. (Ibid. fol. 199.)

tion of the Kingdom with the Holy See, to acquaint him with the whole state of affairs, and to get his full and solemn confirmation of all that his Legate, Cardinal Pole, had done up till then.

From the same document we gather the following fact—very much to our purpose. The embassy consisted of Bishop Thirlby and of two gentlemen, Anthony Montague and Edward Carne. Of the first Paul IV. says:[1] "the Bishop pleaded like a man of genuine eloquence and sound learning"[2] in the pontifical presence. He, then, and his two companions, both in word and in writing, explained how greatly the full reconciliation of the Church of England with that of Rome was desired, and besought in particular for a confirmation of those dispensations whereby *ecclesiastical* personages, whether secular or religious, could be *promoted to the Orders* as well as to the benefices, *invalidly obtained* by them during the schism.[3] This clause in the Summary is most important, for it completely refutes the charge so confidently brought against the *Apostolicae Curae* of having misinterpreted the meaning of the distinction in the Bull of Julius III. (see above), between the *promoti* and *non promoti*. In this Summary Pole states the matters in regard to which he desires a ratification of his action from Paul IV. But the dispensation grants which he had given and thus seeks to have ratified, were given in virtue of the powers imparted to him by Julius III. As the ratification he desired was in every particular, according to the terms of his Summary,

---

[1] *Epistola Pauli IV., Philippo et Maria Angliae Regibus, June 30, 1555.* Cf. Tierney's Dodd "History of the Church," II, p. 120; *Documenta ad Leg. Poli spectantia*, pp. 24-26.

[2] *Oravit* Episcopus vera eloquentia et sana praeditus doctrina.

[3] "Dispensationes cum *ecclesiasticis* personis, saecularibus et diversorum ordinum, *ut promoveantur tam in ordinibus*, quam beneficiis obtentis *nulliter* sub schismate."

granted him in the *Praeclara Carissimi*, the corresponding clauses in Pole's Summary, his letters to the Queen, and his faculties granted to his suffragans, the Bull of Julius III. and the Bull of Paul IV. must all bear the same meaning, and can be used to interpret one another. Nay, taken together they unquestionably distinguish between Orders given by the Catholic, and Orders given by the Edwardine, form, and treat the latter as null and void.

Unless we suppose that this request was wholly without meaning, it follows that in the opinion of the ambassadors there were at that time in England certain ecclesiastics who, during the schism, had been invalidly ordained. That these were no other than such as had been ordained with the new rite of Edward VI. is deducible, not merely from the fact that it was in regard to such alone that the Legate had till then, and did afterwards avail himself of his dispensing power, but also from the notorious fact that the ambassadors, in order to prove the need and urgency of their request, brought with them to Rome the very text of the *Ordinal* wherewith the said ecclesiastics had been ordained during the schism, and submitted it to the examination of the Holy See.[1]

All doubt on this point—if reasonable doubt could yet remain—must vanish on reading the following decree of Queen Mary, of whom these ambassadors were the honorable representatives and faithful interpreters at Rome:[2] "As to those who have already been promoted to any kind of Orders according to the newly fabricated method of ordaining, seeing that truly and *de facto* they have not been ordained at all, the Diocesan Bishop, if he finds

---

[1] Arch. Vatic. Nuntiatura di Inghilterra m. 103. Cf. Bibliotheca Pia. 240.

[2] *Doc ad Poli leg. spect. p 4.*

them fit and worthy, may supply what was wanting in the said persons."[1]

Orders and Benefices "Nulliter et de Facto."

Among the modern defenders of the validity of Anglican Orders an isolated attempt has been made to weaken the force of Paul IV.'s declaration in reply to the ambassadors, by assuming that the Pope, having but recently entered upon the Pontificate, could not have accurately examined the question, and therefore did not intend to decide it in his Bull of June 20, 1555, or else decided it without mature deliberation.[2]

It is needless seriously to argue this assertion, since we have the word of the Pontiff himself assuring us in express terms, that he sanctioned no request made to him by the ambassadors of Mary and Philip except after careful and diligent inquiry: "Praemissis omnibus," he writes in the same Bull, "cum nonnullis ex fratribus Nostris ipsius Romanae Ecclesiae Cardinalibus, *propositis et diligenter discussis, habitaque desuper deliberatione matura,* singula (idest) dispensationes, decreta, etc. . . . auctoritate apostolica *ex certa scientia* approbamus et confirmamus."

[1] "Circa illos qui iam promoti fuere ad aliquos ordines *secundum modum ordinandi noviter fabricatum,* considerando quod *vere et de facto ordinati non fuerunt,* Episcopus Dioecesanus, si illos idoneos et capaces invenerit, supplere potest id quod antea in illis hominibus defuit."

[2] *Bul'a Secreta Pauli IV.* "Praeclara carissimi." Archiv. Vatic. *Regesta Pontificum,* n. 1850, Tom. 46, f. 55. As England remained without Catholic bishops for the long period of 66 years, it is not surprising that this Bull, which referred to England, was forgotten However, it has happily and providentially come to light in good time. Our readers will remember that no sooner was it found after long and diligent search amid the Bulls and Acts relating to the Council of Trent where it had been inserted, than the *Civiltà Cattolica* at once announced the discovery, and published the most important part of it in its issue of June 1, 1895.

Now, among the "dispensationes" was precisely the one just referred to, which concerned ecclesiastics *ut promoveantur in beneficiis et ordinibus nulliter obtentis sub schismate.* Paul IV. approves and confirms it, adding to it this clause : "Ita tamen ut si qui ad ordines ecclesiasticos tam sacros quam non sacros ab alio quam episcopo aut archiepiscopo *rite et recte ordinato* promoti fuerunt, *eosdem ordines ab eorum ordinario de novo suscipere teneantur,* nec interim in iisdem ordinibus ministrent."[1]

Therefore Paul IV. recognizes that there were some in England at that time who *de facto* had received during the schism not only ecclesiastical benefices, but also Orders which were invalid. In this sense Leo XIII. observes rightly in his Bull : "Neque praetermittendus est locus ex eisdem Pontificis (Pauli IV.) litteris, omnino rei congruens ; ubi cum aliis beneficio dispensationis egentibus numerantur qui *tam ordines quam beneficia ecclesiastica nulliter et de facto obtinuerant.*"[2]

Nor is this all. For with the same apostolic authority Paul IV. confirms and approves all that had been decreed by his Legate, Cardinal Pole, about these ordinations. "Eadem apostolica auctoritate . . ea

---

1 In such sort, however, that if any were promoted to ecclesiastical Orders, holy or other, by a bishop or archbishop not duly and rightly ordained, they shall be obliged to receive the same Orders again from their Ordinary and meanwhile to abstain from exercising the ministry of those Orders.

2 In thus quoting from the *Praeclara carissimi* Leo XIII. has been charged very confidently by the Anglican press with adulterating the words of his predecessor—that is, by omitting the word *concernentia,* and thereby making the words *nulliter et de facto* apply to the Orders themselves, instead of to dispensations granted and made in connection with them. Leo XIII. presumably omitted this word because there is some doubt about the reading, and the experts say its admission into the text, or omission from it, makes no difference. See on this point an excellent article in the *Tablet,* of October 17, 1896. (p. 606).

omnia quae praedictus Reginaldus Cardinalis Legatus decrevit, *decernimus*, necnon omnibus his quibus ipse robur Apostolicae firmitatis adiecit Nos quoque robur ipsum adiicimus." But Cardinal Pole had decreed[1] that those who were wrongly ordained—*male ordines susceperunt*—could not be held capable of the sacred ministry until duly reordained, and that, therefore, those who had been ordained with the new rite of Edward VI. *non servata forma et intentione Ecclesiae*, must be regarded as *invalidly* ordained. Therefore Paul IV., by his apostolic authority confirmed, approved and decreed anew, that *ordinations performed with the new Anglican rite should be accounted invalid and null*.

The Bull of Paul IV. was brought to England by the aforementioned Bishop Thirlby, and was published by Cardinal Pole, Sept. 22, 1555, as appears from a note in Pole's handwriting in his Register, which is in the public Archives at Douay.

The Bishops' "Rite et Recte non Ordinati."

Then a doubt arose in the mind of some concerning the schismatical bishops, whether they should be accounted as *rite et recte ordinati*, or not. To this doubt the same Pontiff replied in a Brief of Oct.[2] following, in which he says: "Nos haesitationem hujusmodi tollere et serenitati conscientiae eorum qui, schismate durante, ad ordines promoti fuerant, mentem et intentionem quam in eisdem litteris Nostris habuimus, clarius exprimendo, opportune consulere volentes,[3] *declaramus eos tantum episcopos et archiepiscopos qui non*

---

[1] See his letter to the Bishop of Norwich.

[2] Arch. Secret. Vatic., *Brev. Origin. Pauli, pp. IV.*, Tom I., n. 301.

[3] "We declare that it is only those bishops and archbishops who have not been ordained and consecrated *in forma Ecclesiae* that cannot be considered duly and rightly ordained."

in forma Ecclesiae ordinati et consecrati fuerunt, rite et recte ordinatos dici non posse. Who, then, were and who must have been these bishops, ordained indeed, but not rightly and duly ordained, because not ordained *in forma Ecclesiae?* Plainly they were not the Catholic bishops ordained with the Catholic Pontifical; nor could they have been the schismatical bishops ordained with the same Pontifical under Henry VIII.; it remains, therefore, that they were the schismatical bishops ordained under Edward VI. with the new rite; since, be it well noted and let us not cease to insist upon it,—at that time there were only two classes of bishops in England,—those ordained with the Catholic *Pontifical* and those ordained with the *Ordinal* of Edward VI.

To this latter class, for example, belonged at least six "bishops" then alive—Poynet, Hooper, Coverdale, Scory, Taylor and Harley, who, as we pointed out before, were certainly consecrated with that *Ordinal* during the last three years of the reign of Edward VI.

"IN FORMA ECCLESIAE CONSUETA."

Certain critics have tried to show that the words *in forma Ecclesiae* used by Paul IV., and the words *in forma Ecclesiae consueta* used by Julius III. might possibly be understood to refer not strictly to the Catholic form or rite of the Pontifical, but to the *essential form* of the Sacrament, which is always the *forma Ecclesiae.* These and other similar conjectures were quite well known to Leo XIII., when he was drawing up his Bull. And for this very reason he notices with admirable clearness and precision that the force of the said words was by no means vague nor left to the determination of individual caprice, but was obviously determined by the scope these two Pontiffs had before them in answering the inquiries which came from England. That scope was not, so to

say, speculative and impertinent to the religious questions of the hour; but entirely practical and altogether adapted to those requirements which had to be met with special rules and instructions, delivered to the Legate—himself a skilled theologian not needing to be taught the elements of theology. " For since the faculties given to the Apostolic Legate by these Popes had reference merely to England and to the state of religion therein, the practical rules, which they delivered in answer to his request, could by no means have been directed to determining the general question as to the requisites for valid ordination, but necessarily concerned the particular point of providing for ordinations in England, under the circumstances and conditions represented as then prevailing."

In the Brief of Julius III., ordinations not made *in forma Ecclesiae* CONSUETA are declared invalid. The particular matter here treated of was, therefore, the ordination conferred with the *new form*, which having been but three years in existence, having been used only in England in a few cases, could not possibly be called the *forma Ecclesiae consueta*. Further, in the particular case of the Brief of Paul IV., if his declaration did not relate expressly to the episcopal ordinations performed during the schism with the Edwardine *Ordinal*, but, as these critics would have it, to the abstract question of the solution of which there was never a doubt, (sc. whether the essential sacramental form was necessary for the validity of ordinations) far from allaying doubt (haesitationem tollere), or smoothing consciences (serenitati conscientiae consulere), he would have done just the contrary. For in a matter so delicate, so fraught with the danger of pernicious error, he would have left it to the private authority of each man to judge for himself whether or not the *essential form* needed for episcopal consecration was preserved in the new *Ordinal*.

Therefore, as under Leo XIII., in 1896, so under Paul IV. in 1555, the doubt, which was examined and solved with reference to certain particular ordinations, concerned most especially the *form* according to which they were conferred. That form was judged by Paul IV. to be substantially different from the *forma Ecclesiae* and therefore all the episcopal ordinations derived from it were pronounced invalid—a fact which is manifestly confirmed by the most practical and important consequence deduced from it by Paul IV. in the same Brief: "And therefore," he concludes, "we declare the persons ordained by those bishops not to have received Orders; and that they ought to and must forthwith receive the same Orders from their Ordinary, according to the content and tenor of Our Letter aforesaid."

In the investigations which Leo XIII. caused to be made preparatory to his Bull, it was furthermore observed (and to our mind not without foundation) that up to the time of Paul IV., owing to the great confusion caused in the English episcopate by Henry VIII., followed by the open heresy under Edward VI., it was not quite evident to all that the ordinations had been invalidated, not merely by defect of form, but also in many cases by the absence of episcopal character in the ordainers, and that this being known to Paul IV., he provided for the need in the restrictive clause quoted above. But be that as it may, it is certain that if episcopal character was lacking in the ordainers, the defect, according to the mind of Paul IV., was to be ascribed to the inherent vice of the *new* form of the Edwardine Ordinal with which they had been consecrated. But, some one may say, if the thing is so very clear as that, how comes it that in the past two years some writers, even Catholics, have stood up for the validity, or at least the doubtful invalidity of Anglican Orders, or have maintained that the question was still open and

untouched? To such an objection we can give no more crushing, and at the same time no more charitable, reply than that of Leo XIII., in his Bull: "Perchance because the documents of the Apostolic See were not as well known as they should have been, one or another Catholic writer has not doubted his liberty to dispute the matter."

THE FOREGOING INTERPRETATION CONFIRMED BY FACTS.

This interpretation of the documents of Julius III. and of Paul IV. is confirmed by the line of action pursued on all occasions by the Legate in the solution of particular cases, and by a host of other facts, which history records, closely connected with their publication in England. This same confirmation is indicated by Leo XIII., in his Bull, with the usual brevity and clearness: "And it was in this sense that the Legate understood the instructions and orders of the Apostolic See, and in this sense that he duly and religiously obeyed them."

Among the many records which fully justify this passage of the Bull, we find two letters of the Cardinal Legate; the first directed to the English Sovereigns Mary and Philip,[1] dated December 24, 1554; the other to the Bishop of Norwich,[2] dated January 29, 1555. In the first, Cardinal Pole declares that he has, in virtue of the faculties conferred on him by the Holy See, already dispensed, and is further prepared to dispense those who, through defect of jurisdiction and relying on the pretended supremacy of the Anglican Church, "had *nulliter et de facto* obtained dispensations, concessions, graces and indults, whether Orders or benefices or other spiritual matters."

But as he himself explicitly adds, this refers *solely* to

[1] Statute 2 of Philip and Mary, c. 8; Doc. ad leg. Poli spect, pp. 31-34.
[2] Pocock's Burnet, v.. vi., p. 361; Doc., etc. pp. 9-12.

that nullity which derives from defect of *jurisdiction—quoad nullitatem ex defectu jurisdictionis prefatae tantum insurgentem.*

But what the Legate himself did, and what his delegates were to do, when the nullity arose not only from defect of jurisdiction, but, further, from invalid ordination, is told us in the other letter. For there His Eminence delegates to the Bishop of Norwich some of the faculties which he himself had received from the Pope, and amongst them that of admitting to the exercise of their Orders (*in suis ordinibus*) those ecclesiastics who had been ordained by schismatical or heretical bishops, provided they had been ordained with the Catholic rite: "*Dummodo in eorum (ordinum) collatione Ecclesiae forma et intentio sit servata.* But if instead, they had been ordained with the *new* Edwardine *Ordinal* (and there were no other rites than these two known in England at that time), then the said ecclesiastics should be regarded as not ordained, and as such *ad omnes etiam sacros et Presbyteratus ordines a suis ordinariis, si digni et idonei reperti fuerint, rite et legitime promoveri.*"

Further, that the Catholic rite, the *Ecclesiae forma et intentio*, of which the Cardinal Legate speaks in this letter of 1555, was precisely the ancient Pontifical is evident from the formal question which had to be put to each of the said ecclesiastics: *Utrum ante octo annos fuerint ordinati,*[1] *i. e.*, whether they had been ordained before the death of Henry VIII. (1547), when the Catholic Pontifical was still in use universally and exclusively.

"Idque pariter factum est a Regina Maria." Queen Mary interpreted the Pontifical documents in precisely the same sense. What Leo XIII. here says is proved historically by the Acts of that Queen. Suffice it to

---

[1] Harleian MSS. 421. In about forty cases the accused are interrogated as to whether their Orders were received "ante octo annos."

recall her celebrated decree, already referred to, against ecclesiastics ordained "*secundum modum ordinandi noviter fabricatum.*"

It is also well known that Mary, authorized by the Legate, deposed from their sees all those "bishops" (Taylor, Harley and the rest) who had been consecrated with the Ordinal of her brother Edward. We have before us the processes of these depositions, together with the reasons on which the sentences were based. Against Taylor we read: *Privatus ob nullitatem consecrationis;* against Harley we read in addition: *Privatus propter coniugium et haeresim; et ut supra,* (*i. e. ob nullitatem consecrationis*).[1]

[1] "The Register of Canterbury, in which all these deprivations are recorded, (*i. e.*, of Holgate of York, consc. 1537; Ferrer of St. David's, consc. 1548; Bird of Chester, cons. 1537; Bush of Bristol, cons. 1542, and also of Taylor of Lincoln, cons. 1552; Hooper of Gloucester, cons. 1551; Harlowe of Hereford, cons. 1553; see Pocock's Burnet, ii. pp. 440--1), testifieth that on the 20th of March, 1554, the Bishops of Winchester, London, Chichester and Durham, by virtue of the Queen's commission directed to them, pronounced the sentence of deprivation upon John Taylor, Bishop of Lincoln, *ob nullitatem consecrationis ejus et defectum tituli quem habuit a Rege Edwardo Sexto, per literas patentes cum hac clausula, dummodo bene se gessent;* upon John Hooper, Bishop of Worcester and Gloucester, *propter conjugium et alia mala merita et vitiosum titulum ut supra;* upon John Harlowe, Bishop of Hereford, *propter conjugium, et haeresim, et ut supra;* upon John Bird, Bishop of Chester, *propter conjugium.* No sentence of deprivation was pronounced at that time upon Bush, Bishop of Bristol. Whether he evaded it by renouncing his marriage, or by any other submission, is uncertain. But he was never deposed. However, willingly or unwillingly, he resigned his bishopric in June following. For in the same Register the Dean and Chapter of Canterbury assumed the spiritual jurisdiction of the See of Bristol, void *per spontaneum resignationem Pauli Bushe,* 1554, June 21."

This extract, given by Pocock as foot-note to Burnet, II, p. 441, is from Antony Harmer's *Specimens of Errors,* p. 133. Antony Harmer is a *nom de plume* assumed by Henry Wharton, the author of *Anglia Sacra,* who in 1693 wrote it under the full title of *A specimen of some errors and defects in the History of the Reformation of the Church of England,* by Antony Harmer.

Similar to the Queen's action was the action of those who, as Leo XIII. says in the same passage, labored with her for the restitution of the Catholic religion to its former ascendency. (*Cum ea dederunt operam ut religio et instituta catholica in pristinum locum restituerentur.*) Let the two illustrious bishops, Gilbert Bourne of Bath and Wells, and Bonner, Pole's chief commissioner for the diocese of London, bear witness for the rest. The former in a letter to his Vicar General, John Cottrell, April 8, 1554, orders him to proceed against the pretended marriages of priests, secular and regular, "nec non in eos laicos conjugatos *qui praetextu et sub velamine presbyteratus ordinis*, sese in juribus ecclesiasticis temere et illicite immiscuerunt ac ecclesias parochiales cum cura animarum et dignitates ecclesiasticas contra sacras canonum sanctiones et jura ecclesiastica de facto assecuti fuerunt," *i. e.*, "and against those married laymen who, under pretence and cover of priestly Order, have audaciously and unlawfully arrogated to themselves ecclesiastical rights, and have, contrary to the sacred canonical sanctions and laws of the Church, obtained *de facto* ecclesiastical dignities and parish churches with the care of souls attached."[1] That these intruders *sub velamine presbyteratus ordinis* were those who had been ordained with the Edwardine rite can hardly be denied, in view of the care taken to ascertain, in such cases as those previously referred to, whether their ordination had taken place at least eight years previously—that is, before the introduction of the Edwardine Ordinal.

Bishop Bonner is still more explicit and writes thus: "These pseudo-ministers (*ministelli*), who were created during the schism, have received, through this newly-forged Ordinal, no power of offering the Body and Blood

---

[1] Harleian, MSS. 6967, f. 58. Cf. Strype, *Eccles. Mem.* Ed. Oxon. v. 352.

of Jesus Christ in the Mass."[1] For the rest it is an indisputable historical fact that in the reign of Mary no bishop or minister ordained with the Edwardine Ordinal was ever admitted by the Legate or by the Papal commissioners Gardiner and Brooks, or by the other Catholic bishops, to the exercise of the Orders conferred upon him by the new rite; that no account whatever was made of such orders ; and that therefore whenever one of the said bishops or ministers was condemned for heresy he was never subjected, like those validly ordained, to the penalty of degradation.

It is true that some critics, following apparently the lead of Dr. Lee, have lately asserted that four bishops, Thirlby, Wharton, Aldrich and King, although consecrated with the Edwardine Ordinal, were rehabilitated and recognized as true bishops by the Legate. But their assertion is plainly shown to be false, since it appears from authentic documents that they had received episcopal consecration according to the rite of the Catholic Pontifical. For as a matter of fact the English Episcopal Registers witness that the whole four were consecrated prior to 1550, when the Edwardine Ordinal was not yet in existence—Thirlby in 1540, Wharton in 1536, Aldrich in 1537, and King in 1536.

The Practice of Reordaining Anglican Bishops and Ministers, since 1555.

To the facts above cited, which the past and present defenders of Anglican Orders have vainly essayed to deny, we must add another which alone would be a full and evident confirmation of the interpretation given in his Bull by Leo XIII. to the Acts of Julius III. and Paul IV. It is as follows : " Under the reign of Mary,

[1] See the Preface to his *Profitable and Necessary Doctrine*, (ap. Estcourt, p. 58).

and from the very day when the Legate published the Bull of Paul IV. in England (Sept. 22, 1555), began the practice, followed without interruption up to our own times not only in England, but in France, in the United States of America, in Papal Rome itself and everywhere, of ordaining as simple laymen without any condition, *de novo et ex integro*, those Anglican bishops and ministers who, having returned to the bosom of the Church, desired to consecrate themselves to the service of the altar."

The ancient episcopal registers, lately examined in England, bear witness to this fact in fourteen distinct cases, whereof eight were in the diocese of London. We are speaking here of ecclesiastics ordained with the Edwardine ritual, who between 1555 and 1558 *de novo et ex integro eosdem ordines susceperunt.*

Dr. Brown, the Anglican Bishop of Stepney, has confirmed and commented on this fact in a recent letter to the London *Times* (May 1, 1896).

On the death of Pole (Nov. 18, 1558), and after the destruction of the Catholic hierarchy in England by Elizabeth, those who had been converted under Mary were forced to seek refuge in other countries from the cruel and persistent persecution which raged against them at home. We find them in France, in Flanders, in Rome and elsewhere. Canon Estcourt, in his classical work already quoted so often,[1] speaking of those who had sought an asylum in France, publishes a list of converted Anglican ministers who were unconditionally reordained in the years 1575, '77, '78, '79, '80, '81, 1601, etc. The same fact is witnessed to by the documents preserved at Rome in the Archives of the Holy Office, and of the English College. From one of these documents—seemingly of 1686—we learn that in Scotland

---

[1] The Question of Anglican Ordinations. London, 1873.

also the same discipline prevailed "of receiving and treating as simple laymen those Anglican and Scottish bishops and priests who returned to the Catholic faith."[1]

Therefore we must reject as historically false the opinion of those few who have recently tried to prove that the said discipline originated, not from the Pontifical Acts of 1553-1555, but only in the year 1704, or in the earlier part of the eighteenth century.[2] It is to this false opinion, if we mistake not, that the following words of the Bull of Leo XIII. refer : " The authorities, which we have quoted from Julius III. and Paul IV., show plainly the origin of that discipline, which has been observed with unbroken continuity for over three centuries, of treating Edwardine ordinations as ineffectual and null ; and to this discipline abundant witness is borne by the record of many of the said ordinations which, even in this very city, have frequently been reiterated unconditionally according to the Catholic rite."

[1] From a *Lettera di Mgr. Francesco Genelli a Mgr. Casoni, Assessore del S. Ufficio.*

[2] It is indeed strange that these critics, taking their stand on a *supposed* decree of the Holy Office in 1704, did not advert to the fact that their assertion is expressly denied in the text of the very decree which they publish. Thus in the text which Gasparri (*De la valeur des Ordinations Anglicanes*, Paris, 1895, pp. 16-18) gives us under the heading " Voici le texte tout entier du décret," we read : " *Constans semper fuit in Anglia praxis* ut si quis haereticorum Ministrorum ad gremium revertatur Ecclesiae *saecularis* instar habeatur. Unde, si ligatus sit matrimonio, in eodem permaneat ; sin liber et ad statum ecclesiasticum transire velit *aliorum catholicorum more ordinetur*, vel, si libuerit, uxorem ducat." ("It has always been the constant practice in England whenever any one of the heretical ministers returned to the bosom of the Catholic Church to treat him as a layman—so that if he was joined in matrimony, he should remain therein, and if he was free and desired to pass into the ecclesiastical state, he should be ordained just like any other Catholic, or if he desired it, he should take a wife.")

The Case of John Gordon.

But if the year 1704 does not mark the beginning of the practice in question, it certainly does mark the beginning of a new series of documents from the Holy See wherein that practice was solemnly confirmed and pronounced obligatory.

For in this year a question was put to the Congregation of the Holy Office touching the Orders received by a certain John C. Gordon, Protestant Bishop of Glasgow, who on his conversion to Catholicism wished to serve the Church in the ecclesiastical state. Gordon, it is to be noted, had been ordained not with the Edwardine *Ordinal* of 1550, on which Julius III. and Paul IV. had pronounced sentence, but with the modified Edwardine Ordinal of 1662. From the *authentic* Acts of the said Congregation it seems that the doubt was proposed to the Consultors for examination on March 10, 1704; and after two weeks they gave their *votum*: "Quod praedictus Johannes Clemens Gordon *ordinetur ex integro*." On Wednesday, the 26th of the same month, "Emi dixerunt quod inclusae scripturae mittantur per manus eorumdem Emorum." What these "inclusae scripturae" were will be seen from the decree, which we quote in full. It is moreover certain that the doubt was discussed and studied from the very beginning for the space of thirty-six days, as well by the Consultors as by their Eminences, the Inquisitors General. The *genuine* decree, whose text is here published for the first time, runs as follows:

"On Thursday (*Feria V.*) the 17th day of April, 1704, in the accustomed Congregation of the H. R. and Universal Inquisition, held in the Palace of St. Peter, in the presence of our Most Holy Lord Clement, Pope, the Eleventh.

"The petition (*instantia*) of John Clement Gordon, an Anglican Bishop, converted to the Catholic faith,

being presented, and (together with it) certain documents or authorities (*juribus*) otherwise collected for the sake of a similar case, although it (the similar case) was not decided, or at least no decree was made in reference to it, together (also) with the *Votum* of the Consultors, by which (petition) he begged that, notwithstanding this episcopal consecration received from Bishops of the Anglican sect, and by the accustomed rite of those pseudo-Bishops, he may be granted leave to pass to the reception of the order of the Priesthood by the Catholic rite, on the ground that his consecration to the episcopate is null, both on account of the want of legitimate succession of the Bishops in England and Scotland who had consecrated him, and also on account of other reasons by which his aforesaid consecration is rendered null.

"The Most Holy (Lord), having heard the *vota* of the Most Eminent Cardinals, decreed that John Clement Gordon be ordained fully and absolutely (*ex integro et absolute*) to all the orders and particularly to that of Priesthood, and, inasmuch as he has not been confirmed, that he first receive the Sacrament of Confirmation."

It is needless to observe that this was not strictly speaking a decree of the Holy Office afterwards confirmed by the Pope, as has been stated and printed during the controversy of the last two years; but was truly a decree emanating from the Pope himself, *Sanctissimus decrevit.*

The "*scripturae et jura alias collecta pro simili casu,*" alluded to in the decree, are the vota and acts of the same Congregation relative to a case proposed to them on the 24th of July, 1684, by the Bishop of Fano, Apostolic Nuncio to Paris. The case was that of "a young Calvinist heretic, who passing from France into England, had there been ordained to the diaconate according to the use of that sect; and afterwards to the pres-

byterate by the pseudo-Bishop of London. Having come back to France and embraced the Catholic faith he now wanted to marry." Were his orders valid so as to constitute an impediment to matrimony?

Of this case the Holy Father writes as follows in his Bull: "After a careful investigation,[1] some of the Consultors gave their answers, or vota as they are called, in writing, and the rest united with them in their sentence *pro invaliditate ordinationis;* yet having respect to the opportuneness of the decision it seemed good to the Cardinals to defer the matter.[2] If, then, a final decision was not given in this case, it was not because their Eminences, the judges of the Supreme Congregation, had any doubt as to the justice of the Consultors' resolution, but for an altogether extrinsic motive, as is plain from contemporary acts, and especially from the vote of Cardinal Casanata, who acted as *Relator*.[3]

Furthermore, from the fact that *eadem acta repetita et ponderata sunt* in Gordon's case, we are enabled to

[1] On that occasion also a special commission was instituted. Mgr. Genetti, who was on it, wrote thus concerning it to the Holy Office in a "Relation" dated April 15, 1704: "The question being of great consequence, and requiring frequently to be acted upon, several Congregations were held to consider it, in which Mgr. Leyborn presided, and seven or eight of the most learned theologians from among the English clergy took part, among whom were Mr. Gifford, afterwards Bishop and Vicar Apostolic, Mr. Bettan, now tutor to the King of England, and other doctors of the Sorbonne and of Douay, all men of professed learning."

[2] The original text of the Consultors' resolution is as follows: Feria II. die 13 Augusti, 1685. DD. CC., mature discusso dubio, unanimi voto responderunt *pro invaliditate praedictae ordinationis.* An autem expediat ad hanc declarationem in praesenti casu devenire EE. PP. oraculo reliquerunt.

[3] In the years 1684 and 1685 England was much disturbed about the religious question, and the Cardinals, abiding by the *vote* of the *Relator*, prudently decided to abstain from an act which then might have created new difficulties for James II. in his endeavors to restore the Catholic religion.

understand the motives on which the decree of Clement XI. was founded. From the number of these motives must be excluded, before all, the legend concerning Parker's consecration. In fact, it is repeatedly insisted in those *Acta* (of 1684—6 and of 1704) that: "In a matter so grave, a resolution of such consequence cannot be rested on a fact contradicted both by Catholics and Protestants;" that "the adequate decision must be drawn, not from the facts of Parker's case, which depended on so entangled a narrative, but from the insufficient intention and words used by the Anglican heretics in the ordering of priests," that "the chief point to discuss was the Edwardine Ordinal, which remained in full vigor for over a hundred years; and the same as somewhat modified under Charles II. in 1662;" that such an examination was made having due regard to the Oriental forms, and that for that reason "the formulas and prayers used by the Armenians, Maronites, Syrians, Jacobites, Nestorians, Catholic and heretical alike, had been then translated and studied;" that, more particularly in 1704, "duobus vel tribus novis *Votis* fuit denuo *demonstrata* nullitas istarum ordinationum, *potissimum* ex insufficientia formae." ("The nullity of these ordinations was demonstrated afresh by two or three new *Vota*, and that, more particularly from the insufficiency of the *form.*") This fact, although expressly stated in the authoritative decree of Clement XI., seems to have escaped the notice of Mr. Lacey, who writes: "There is no trace of any independent inquiry at the time when the Gordon case actually came on." (*Guardian*, Dec. 9, 1896, p. 1982.) Whence it appears how justly the Holy Father observes, that although the Anglican Bishop Gordon himself in his *pro-memoria* enumerates the Parkerian legend among the causes of the nullity of his own consecration, nevertheless *in sententia ferenda omnino seposita est ea causa*

ut documenta produnt integrae fidei, neque alia ratio est reputata nisi defectus formae et intentionis. ("*In the delivery of the decision this reason was altogether set aside, as documents of incontestable authenticity prove, nor was any weight whatever attached to any other reason than that of the defect of form and intention.*") And if, in the exposition of the case which is reported in the genuine text of the decree, express mention is made of the defect of legitimate episcopal succession, such defect is to be reduced to that of invalidity of form, by which the bishops being spurious the succession deriving from them must also be spurious, as Paul IV. had already decided, and as was explicitly stated in the *relation* introductory to the decree.

From the same *Acts*, concerning the two cases examined by the Holy Office in 1684-6 and 1704,[1] it is equally evident that, if the question of the *traditio instrumentorum*, which has no place in the Anglican Ordinal, was touched upon, it was not in order to prove an essential defect, but only to show "if this *also* was wanting, then *all* determination of the words used in the *form*, all specification of the *power* to be conferred was likewise wanting." For what theologian does not know that, even at that time, according to the jurisprudence of the Holy Office,[2] such a defect was not considered a certain proof of nullity, and, therefore, as the Holy Father says in his Bull: "Tunc praescriptum de more erat ut ordinatio *sub conditione* instauraretur?" ("It was at that time prescribed by custom that the ordination should be repeated conditionally.")

Finally, it must be observed that although the decree of Clement XI. has reference to the particular case of

[1] The same must be said of the *Acta* in the subsequent cases examined by the same Congregation, down to that laid before it in 1874 by the Archbishop of Westminster.

[2] Cf. Arch. S. O. *De Ordinibus Sacris*, from 1603 to 1699.

Gordon, nevertheless it was not based on a reason peculiar to that case alone, but on a general reason, namely, *vitium formae*, which affects equally all orders conferred by the same form. In an ancient document of the Holy Office it is noted expressly: Summus Pontifex pronuntiavit judicium *directe* quidem de facto in casu speciali proposito, *indirecte* vero de jure generali invaliditatis Ordinum Anglicanorum. ("The Pope passed judgment, directly, indeed, as to the fact in the particular case under consideration; but indirectly as to the general question of the validity of Anglican Orders.") The Sacred Congregation, ruling itself by this interpretation and confirming it by its subsequent *Acts*, has always, in dealing with similar cases, answered by quoting and applying the Decree of Clement XI.

Therefore, the practice of ordaining *ex integro* and unconditionally those ordained with the Anglican rite has been constantly observed in the Church from 1555 to 1704, and thence to our own days—*i. e.*, for three centuries and a half. The thirty-four Popes, who during that interval have occupied the Chair of Peter, have not been ignorant of the existence of this practice and have not only tolerated, but formally sanctioned and approved it. Whence we deduce the following weighty theological argument : "Quoniam," says the Holy Father in his Bull, "firmum semper ratumque in Ecclesia mansit, ordinis sacramentum nefas esse iterari, fieri nullo pacto poterat ut talem consuetudinem Apostolica Sedes pateretur tacita ac toleraret. Atqui eam non toleravit solum sed probavit etiam et sancit ipsa, quotiescumque in eadem re peculiare aliquod factum incidit judicandum." ("Since in the Church it has ever been a constant and established rule that it is sacrilegious to repeat the Sacrament of Orders, it never could have come to pass that the Apostolic See should have silently acquiesced in and tolerated such a custom. But not only did the

Apostolic See tolerate this practice, but approved and sanctioned it as often as any particular case arose which called for its judgment in the matter.")

Such is, so to say, the *extrinsic* argument against the validity of Anglican Orders. But this is not the only, nor the principal one on which Leo XIII. has based his sentence. There still remains the intrinsic argument, to which we must now turn our attention.

PART III.

DEFECT OF FORM AND INTENTION.

In the preceding paragraphs a study of the Pontifical documents, and of the decree of the Holy Office, relative to Anglican Orders, assured us as to the mind of the Popes, and the constant practice of the Holy See in that matter, from the first examination of the question in 1553 up to our own days. The clear and irrefragable conclusion of our study is that which we read in the Bull of Leo XIII. : "*Controversiam temporibus nostris excitatam Apostolicae Sedis judicio definitam multo antea fuisse.*" This authoritative declaration from the infallible teacher of the Church, and faithful guardian of her divinely instituted sacraments, would have been more than enough to put an end to the unseasonable polemics which were engaging the minds of certain Catholic writers. But the Holy Father, in his paternal solicitude and enlightened wisdom, wished to do still more: "Quoniam," he writes, "nihil nobis antiquius optatiusque est quam ut hominibus recte animatis maxima possimus indulgentia et caritate prodesse, ideo jussimus in Ordinale Anglicanum, quod caput est totius causae, rursus quam studiosissime inquiri." To the extrinsic he has chosen to add an intrinsic argument, thus making our assent to his august decision reasonable on two independent titles, first on account of the supreme and infallible authority from which it comes; secondly by reason of the objective evidence which manifests its

intrinsic truth. Such evidence is derived from the Edwardine *Ordinal* itself, which, being examined both internally and in the light of its historic surroundings, displays two essential defects which vitiate all orders conferred by it—absence of valid *form;* and of due *intention.*

The Ceremony and the Essential Rite of the Sacrament.

In the rite of ordination, as in that of the other sacraments, one must distinguish accurately the *ceremonial* from the *essential* part. The former is mutable and required only for *lawfulness*, the latter immutable and necessary for *validity;* the former is of ecclesiastical, the latter of divine institution. In the essential part it is also usual to distinguish two elements—matter and form. The matter is the sensible thing made use of. The form consists of the words which determine and raise that sensible thing to the nature and power of an *effectual* sign of grace—*i. e.*, both to signify and to produce a definite, internal, spiritual effect. The matter of the Sacrament, according to the analogy of physical composition, is always with respect to the form the determinable and perfectible element, while the form is that which determines and perfects it. Thus in Baptism, which the Apostle defines as *Lavacrum aquae in verbo vitae*, the washing with water is the sensible thing used, or the *matter;* but to this must be joined the word of life, or the *form*, which determines what this washing means, and together with it constitutes the entire sacramental symbol, which has the specific power of cleansing and sanctifying the soul.

What is true of Baptism is true of Orders and of all the Sacraments of the New Law. In all, according to St. Augustine's well-known *dictum: Accedit verbum ad*

elementum et fit sacramentum.[1] St. Thomas Aquinas, speaking in general of the *form* of the sacraments, expresses himself thus: "In all things that are made up of matter and form the determining principle is the form, for whose sake the matter may be said to exist and by which it is brought to its perfection; and, therefore, of the two requisites for the existence of the composition, determined form is more principal than determined matter; . . . and so, since in the sacraments there are required certain sensible things which are, as it were, the matter of the sacraments, *far more requisite is a definite form of words.*"[2]

In other words, since it is the proper function of the sacramental form to limit the matter of the sacrament to a particular signification, it is necessary that the words of which the said form is made up should exactly express the thing to be signified. For the *form* being an intrinsic cause, or constitutive element, exerts its causality by sharing its own nature with and joining it to that of the *matter*. "Forma per se ipsam facit rem esse in actu, cum per essentiam suam sit actus," the form by giving itself (*i. e.*, not by effecting something outside itself), causes the composite thing to be of a determined nature; for it is in itself essentially of a determined nature.[3]

If, therefore, the words of which the sacramental form consists have not of themselves a definite signification, they cannot possibly by their union with a sensible element (or matter) of equally indefinite meaning constitute an *effectual* (*practicum*) *symbol*, which at once signifies that definite grace which it produces, and produces that definite grace which it signifies. Whence arises

---

[1] Tract. LXXX, in Joan. n. 3. Migne, P. L. XXXV, p. 1840.
[2] Summa Th. III, p. q. 60, a 7.
[3] Summa, I. p., q. 76, a. 7.

the absolute necessity of having in each sacrament a definite form peculiar to itself.¹

THE WANT OF A SPECIFICALLY DETERMINED FORM.

And this is true in a very special manner of the Sacrament of Orders, whose *matter*, as the Anglicans themselves allow, consists in the laying-on of hands. But this sign is not unambiguous, nor does it of itself signify some one definite grace. In fact, it is common to the three orders—Episcopate, Priesthood and Diaconate—and is also used in the Sacrament of Confirmation. In order, therefore, that it may signify the grace of Ordination, rather than that of Confirmation, and that in the Sacrament of Ordination it may signify the grace of Episcopacy rather than that of Priesthood or Diaconate, it needs a further determination which, as we said above, can only be derived from the *form* which signifies the gift, the power, or the order which is to be conferred.²

Now, it is just in the want of this determination that we find the first, though not the only *defectus formae*, which has vitiated all the Orders conferred with the Edwardine Ordinal, substituted for the Catholic Pontifical in 1550. Take, for example, the form prescribed for the consecration of bishops, which, according to the undoubted opinion of the compilers of the Ordinal, is

[1] Such is the doctrine briefly but clearly mentioned and asserted by Leo XIII. in his Bull: "All know that the Sacraments of the New Law, as sensible and efficient signs of invisible grace, ought both to signify the graces which they effect, and effect the graces which they signify. Although this signification ought to be found in the whole essential rite—that is to say, in the matter and form—it still pertains chiefly to the form, since the matter is a part which is not determined by itself, but which is determined by the form."

[2] In other words, the laying-on of hands symbolizes a transmission or giving, but in no way specifies the gift transmitted.

as follows: "Accipe Spiritum Sanctum, et memento ut resuscites gratiam Dei quae in te est per manuum impositionem. Non enim dedit nobis Deus spiritum timoris sed virtutis et dilectionis et sobrietatis."

The whole substance of this form is found in the first three words, *Accipe Spiritum Sanctum*, which of themselves have absolutely no fixed specific meaning; they express merely an invocation of the Holy Ghost which, together with the laying-on of hands, might be found in any Sacrament.[1] Nor can it be said that their signification is determined by the words which follow, "ac memento, etc.," since plainly they do not hint at, much less express, the conveyance of any specifically determined grace, being rather an admonition to the elect to stir up a grace which he has already received—viz., "by the laying-on of hands." So, when St. Paul wrote these words to Timothy,[2] he did not thereby confer Ordination upon him, but supposed that he had been already ordained. Nor indeed can it be said that the Apostle there alludes *determinately* to the grace of Episcopate, since the contrary interpretation of those who, following the Council of Trent,[3] apply the said

---

[1] It is plain from the abundant testimony of the Fathers, and notably of St. Cyprian (Epist. 69, 11; 72, 2), that in the reconciliation of public sinners and the re-admission of heretics into the Church, the bishop or priest was wont to lay his hands upon them, in order to impart to them the Holy Ghost, who is the *remissio peccatorum* and the *vinculum unitatis et pacis*. (Thalhofer, Liturgik, 1883, I, p. 646.)

[2] Epist. II. ad Timoth I. 6.

[3] "Whereas, by the testimony of Scripture, by Apostolic tradition and the unanimous consent of the Fathers, it is clear that grace is conferred by sacred ordination, which is performed by words and outward signs, no one ought to doubt that Order is truly and properly one of the Seven Sacraments of Holy Church. For the Apostle says: 'I admonish thee that thou stir up the grace of God, which is in thee by the imposition of my hands. For God has not given us the spirit of fear, but of power and of love and of sobriety.'" (Sess. xxiii, chap. 3.)

words to the Sacrament of Orders in general, is well known.

If, then, we hold that for the validity of Ordination, as for that of every other Sacrament, it is necessary, before all things, that the form should be specifically determined in itself, we must also hold that Anglican Orders conferred with the forms of the Edwardine Ordinal, not thus determined, are null and void.

The Different Forms in the Liturgies of the Church.

The need of having a *form* specifically determined in itself is deduced not merely *a priori*, from the philosophical conception of a *form*, but also *a posteriori*, from the fact that there never has been any form used in the Church, and accepted by her as valid, which did not at least make express mention, either of the Order, or else of the power, to be conferred. We say "at least" in order to make it clear that the determination required for a valid form is not necessarily an explicit mention of both one and the other, much less a mention of the *principal effect* of the Order conferred. If, together with the indication of the Order of power, there is also expressed the principal effect, as in some forms, so much the better; but if this is simply omitted, *and not deliberately excluded*, the argument remains in all its force.

In order briefly and clearly to prove what has just been asserted, we will here give a *conspectus*[1] of the forms of consecration accompanying the laying-on of

---

[1] For the texts of the Liturgies quoted see Assemani, *Codex Liturgicus Eccles. Universae*, Tomi VIII., IX., XI; *Bibliotheca Orientalis*, Tom. III. Morin, *De Sacris Eccles. Ordinationibus;* Denzinger, *Ritus Orientalium;* Duchesne, *Origines du culte Chrétien;* Haskell, *Monumenta Ritualia, etc., etc.*

Defect of Form and Intention.

hands found in the different liturgies recognized by the Church:

LITURGIES		For the Diaconate.	For the Priesthood.	For the Episcopate.
Old Roman		We pray Thee, O Lord, also mercifully to look down on this Thy servant whom we humbly dedicate to the office of DEACON, that he may serve at Thy altars.	Bestow, we beseech Thee, O Lord, on these Thy servants the dignity of the PRESBYTERATE.	And we therefore pray thee, O Lord, to bestow grace upon these Thy servants whom Thou hast chosen to the ministry of the HIGH PRIESTHOOD— (Summi Sacerdotii).
Greek		. . . Do Thou Thyself, O Lord, preserve in all honesty of faith this person whom it has pleased Thee through me to promote to the office of a DEACON, and who holds the sacrament with a pure conscience. Grant (him) the grace granted to STEPHEN the martyr, who was the first called by Thee to the work of this ministry.	O God . . . who hast honored with the designation of PRESBYTER those who have been marked out as worthy to minister the word of Thy truth holily in that degree, Do Thou, Lord of all things, grant in Thy good pleasure, that this person, whom it has pleased Thee that I should promote . . . may in blameless conversation receive the grace of Thy Holy Spirit.	Do Thou, Lord of all things, confirm and strengthen this Thine elect, that, through the hands of me, a sinner, and of the ministers and bishops present, he may by the coming power, and grace of the Holy Spirit, receive the EPISCOPAL DIGNITY.

Syro-Maronite.

Do Thou, O Lord, in this hour look upon Thy servant and send down into him the grace of the Holy Spirit ... and as Thou didst grant grace to *blessed* STEPHEN, the first whom Thou didst call to this MINISTRY, so grant that help from heaven may come down upon this Thy servant.

Choose him by Thy grace and by Thy mercy promote this Thy servant, who on account of Thy manifold kindness and the gift of Thy grace, is presented to-day from the order of deacons to the high and sublime grade of PRESBYTERS.

Do Thou, who canst do all things, adorn also with all good qualities and virtues this Thy servant, whom Thou hast made worthy to receive from Thee the sublime ORDER OF BISHOPS.

Nestorian.

Lord God ... who has chosen Thy Church and hast raised up in it Prophets and Apostles and Priests and Doctors ... and hast likewise placed in it DEACONS and as Thou didst choose STEPHEN and his companions, so now also, O Lord, .. grant to these Thy servants the grace of Thy Holy Spirit, that they may be elected DEACONS.

Do Thou, therefore, great God of virtues ... look down also now upon these Thy servants and choose them by Thy holy election through the indwelling of the Holy Spirit ... and choose them to the PRIESTHOOD.

Do Thou, O Lord, even now cause Thy face to shine on this Thy servant, and choose him by a holy election through the unction of the Holy Spirit, that he may be to Thee a PERFECT PRIEST, ... and confirm him by the Holy Spirit in THIS holy ministry to which he is ascending.

Defect of Form and Intention. 91

<table>
<tr><td rowspan="2">ARMENIAN</td><td>Grant him, O Lord, the power and grace of **HOLY STEPHEN**, Thy Protomartyr and **FIRST DEACON**, that being filled with Thy Holy Spirit, he may abide immaculate in the ministry of Thy holy table.</td><td>Listen, O Lord, now also to the voice of our supplications, and preserve him in this **PRIESTHOOD** to which he has been called, this Thy servant, now ordained, whom Thou hast chosen and received into the **PRESBYTERATE**.</td><td>The Divine Grace calls this N. from the Priesthood to the **EPISCOPATE** ... I lay hands upon him: Pray all that he may be made worthy to preserve the grade of his **EPISCOPATE** immaculate.</td></tr>
</table>

The same *explicit* determination is found also in the consecratory forms of the ancient *Gallican Liturgy*, of the Jacobite Liturgy of Alexandria, of the Syro-Jacobite, of the Coptic and in that of the *Apostolic Constitutions*. Such a constant and uniform fact is admitted by all, even by those few Catholic writers who, prior to the Bull of Leo XIII., more or less patronized the Anglican cause. The illustrious Mgr. Gasparri writes thus: "All the (consecratory) prayers used or approved of by the Church are: 1st, all prayers relating to ordination; 2ndly, they all call down upon the candidate the graces from Heaven necessary for his new state; 3dly, they all *name, in one way or the other, the order in question.* Abbé Boudinhon was equally explicit, in October 1895. In his opinion: "All the Catholic formularies of ordination are framed after one uniform pattern." Now, this pattern always contains an express mention of the order or power to be conferred. As a matter of fact it would be, in his opinion, somewhat as follows: "Deus qui .... respice propitius super hunc famulum tuum quem

ad *Diaconatum* (respective: *Presbyteratum* vel *Episcopatum* seu *Summum Sacerdotium*) vocari dignatus es; da ei gratiam tuam ut munera *huius ordinis* digne et utiliter adimplere valeat."

No Conformity in the Edwardine Ordinal.

This being admitted, we understand still better what the *defectus formae* is, by reason of which the Orders conferred by the Edwardine *Ordinal* are null and void. In the *forms*, therein prescribed for the ordination of priests and the consecration of bishops, there is an absence of all conformity to the *essential type* constantly and universally followed in the Eastern and Western Liturgies. For whereas these latter are always *precatory* and specifically determined, the former are without exception *imperative*, and contain no sort of specific determination of the order, nor of the power, nor of the principal effect.

This assertion needs no further proof. The Anglicans themselves recognized its truth when, in 1662, under Charles II., they partly modified their forms. Thus in the one above quoted they added to the words *Accipe Spiritum Sanctum* these: *in officium et opus Episcopi in Ecclesia Dei*. But as this modification, introduced a hundred and three years after the consecration of Parker, and a hundred and twelve after the abolition of the Catholic Pontifical, could not validate past ordinations which had been invalidated by defect of form, so neither could it validate future ones, which remained, and always will remain, invalid at least by defect of *character* in the ordainer, since they are conferred by pseudo bishops, who are in fact laymen. Hence the Bull of Leo XIII. justly observes: "This same addition, even were it sufficient to complete the *necessary signification of the form*, was introduced too late—

Defect of Form and Intention.

namely, a century after the reception of the Edwardine Ordinal, when by reason of the extinction of the hierarchy the *power of ordaining no longer existed.*" In other words, the remedy, if the modification of 1662 can be so called, was applied too late; *cum mala per longas invaluere moras.*

ANGLICANS SHIFTING THE ARGUMENT.

And so indeed the defenders of the Edwardine *Ordinal* past and present have themselves understood the matter, always setting aside the aforesaid modification, and basing their thesis on other arguments. Among them are to be found some who deny that the designation of the order or power to be conferred is necessary for the validity of the consecratory form; for example, the Anglicans, Messrs. Lacey and Puller, to whose opinion the Abbé Boudinhon showed himself inclined, in July, 1896,[1] thus reversing his conclusion of October, 1895.

It will be enough here to quote the words of Mr. Lacey, copied from Mr. Puller, and approved by the Abbé Boudinhon: "I answer," he writes,[2] "that the mention of the order is not absolutely necessary, . . . for in the *Canons of Hippolytus* there are found prayers for the conferring of orders in the Roman Church, used seemingly in the second or third century, of which *that assigned to the Diaconate contains no mention whatever of the order.*" We will not delay to inquire if the Canons are truly assigned to St. Hippolytus, or if they go back to the second or third century, or if their origin is to be sought in Rome and the West, and not rather in the East; nor shall we endeavor to ascertain the precise

---

[1] *Revue Anglo-Romaine*, July 14.
[2] *Dissertationis Apologeticae de Hierarchia Anglicana Supplementum*, Roma, 1896, page 20.

accuracy of their text, which is quoted by Mr. Lacey in a Latin translation made from a German version, not, indeed, of the original, which is not to be found, but of an Arabic translation of another translation presumed to be Coptic. All these points have been and are so much in dispute among the learned that it seems to be inexcusable frivolity, not to say audacity, to oppose a doubtful passage of certain Canons, probably apocryphal or interpolated, to the indisputable testimony of all the authentic liturgies of East and West.

But in order to show the groundlessness of Mr. Lacey's assertion we need only confront it with what the said Canons of Hippolytus do really say. Here is the fifth: "If a Deacon is to be ordained let the proper canons be observed; and let this prayer be said over him, for it has reference not to the priesthood, but to the *diaconate*, as it befits the minister of God. Let him minister to the bishop and the priests in all things. For the *Deacon* is such an one as he of whom Christ said: 'If any man will minister to me my Father will honor him.' Let the Bishop lay his hands *upon him* and recite this prayer *over him* saying: 'O God, the Father of our Lord Jesus Christ, we earnestly beseech Thee to pour Thy Holy Spirit upon Thy servant N. and to make him ready together with those who, like *Stephen*, minister to Thee according to Thy will. . . . Receive his *ministry* [or diaconate] through our Lord Jesus Christ.'"

With these words before him, and remembering that in all the Oriental Liturgies the Order of Diaconate is expressed in the form by a reference to the protomartyr Stephen, the first deacon, ordained by the Apostles themselves, let the reader judge of the truth of Mr. Lacey's assertion: "In the Canons of Hippolytus . . . the prayer assigned to the diaconate makes *no mention whatever* of the grade to be conferred."

Defect of Form and Intention. 95

Furthermore, according to the same Achelis[1] on whom Mr. Lacéy relies, there is a strict relation of parentage between the pretended Canons of Hippolytus and the Eighth Book of the Apostolic Constitutions, the latter being largely a copy of the former. Now, in this very Eighth Book, the Apostolic Constitutions contain the following consecratory prayer for the diaconate :[2] "Almighty God, show Thy face upon this Thy servant whom Thou hast chosen to the ministry (*ΔΙΑΚΟΝΙΑΝ*), and fill him, as Thou didst fill the protomartyr *Stephen*, with power and the Holy Ghost." The word *ministerium*, used in the Constitutions, corresponds undoubtedly to the word *servitium* in the translation from the German version of the Canons: but *ministerium* is simply the Latin for διακονια. In both alike this *ministerium*, or, if you prefer it, *servitium*, is more than sufficiently determined; for it is specified as the ministry of Stephen, namely, the Diaconate. Let us observe, in concluding, that as regards the two consecratory forms which we are here dealing with, prescribed in the same Canons[3] for priesthood and episcopate, there is no question whatever. In specifically mentioning the order to be conferred they conform exactly to the type of all the other liturgies.

Therefore from the Canons of Hippolytus not only can no serious difficulty be brought against the doctrine of the Bull of Leo XIII., but, contrariwise, they con-

---

[1] Die Canones Hippolyti, p. 27.

[2] Sanc. Apost. Constit., lib. VIII., c. III., *De Mystico Ministerio*, p. 52. J. P. Pitra, op. cit.

[3] See the text in Achelis, op. cit. can. III. and IV., pp. 42 and foll. In the form for the Episcopate we read: "Grant him also, O Lord, the *Episcopate* and a merciful spirit and power," a. s. f.; for the priesthood the rubric says: "The same prayer is said over him (the priest) as over the Bishop, with the sole exception of the word *Episcopate*." (Ibid n. 31, p. 61.)

firm it, and furnish an invincible argument against the sufficiency and validity of the vague and undetermined forms of the Edwardine *Ordinal.*

NO ARGUMENT TO BE DRAWN FROM THE COPTIC RITE.

More specious though not more serious is the reason advanced by certain Anglican ritualists in defence of the sufficiency of their Ordinal, which is founded on an imaginary Decree, wherein the Holy Office is supposed to have declared for the validity of the Coptic priesthood albeit conferred, as in the Anglican Ordinal, by the laying-on of hands accompanied only by the undetermined form: *Accipe Spiritum Sanctum.*

The Decree alluded to is dated April 9, 1704, and is as follows: "The ordination of a priest by the laying-on of hands and the pronouncing of the form *Accipe Spiritum Sanctum*, as described in the *Dubium*, is valid, but the ordination of a deacon by simply imposing the patriarchal cross is altogether invalid."[1]

Supposing this decree to be genuine, and supposing further that it is to be understood to mean that the

---

[1] For the better understanding of the case in question we take the following particulars from the Authentic Acts of the Archives of the Holy Office. (Fasc. xiii, fol. 140, et sqq.). On Oct. 20, 1703, the Sacred Congregation of the Propaganda sent up to the Holy Office six *dubia* proposed by the Most Rev. P. Guiseppe di Gerusalemme, Prefect Apostolic of the Missions of Ethiopia, of which the second was as to "whether an Abyssinian priest or monk is rightly ordained, and consequently whether on becoming a Catholic he can be or ought to be admitted to the exercise of his orders." Their Eminences, Judges of the Holy Office, appointed tne Consultor Giovanni Damasceno "ut refeiat et sententiam suam exprimat de quaesitis." The Consultor obeyed and answered the inquiry as follows: "*Quatenus Aethiopes Jacobitarum vel alio ritu utantur*, in quo eorum sacerdotes seu monachi per manuum impositionem ordinentur, eorum ordinatio est valida. . . ." This *votum* was referred *coram SSmo.*, on Feb. 14, 1704, (Feria V), but was not approved by His Holiness. The Pope's answer is thus reported by the Assessor: "The Pontiff orders

Defect of Form and Intention. 97

three words there quoted, alone constituted the adequate form for the ordering of priests, it is quite intelligible that these Anglicans should, with a certain appearance of truth, accuse the Holy See of self-contradiction by having in 1896 condemned as insufficient for Anglican ordinations the same form which, in 1704, it admitted as sufficient for Coptic ordinations.

But both suppositions are absolutely false. First of all, it is false that the text which they quote is a genuine decree of the Holy Office, from whose authentic *Acts* it is manifest not only that no such decree ever existed, but also that the proposition having been made by a certain *Consultor* under diverse forms, Pope Clement XI. on two several occasions expressly refused to approve it.[1]

---

me to inquire from P. Giuseppi, and from *others versed in the rights of the Abyssinians,* by what *form* the Sacred Orders and the priesthood are conferred by the schismatical Bishops of Ethiopia, and then that the question be formulated and proposed anew." The new *quaesitum* was prepared and set forth in the following terms: " In Ethiopia since the candidates for ordination have come from places far apart in order to be ordained in the city where the schismatical Archbishop resides, and since the latter will only ordain when from eight to ten thousand are gathered for ordination in the said city, it happens at times that he will ordain three or four thousand in one day. The candidates for priesthood being drawn up in lines in the church, the Archbishop passing rapidly in front of them lays his hand on the head of each and says : '*Accipe Spiritum Sanctum ;*' and upon the head of the candidates for diaconate he simply lays his episcopal cross, and since, by reason of the great crowd and the confusion and the rate he goes at, it happens that with some he omits the laying-on of hands; with others, the words of the form ; and both one and the other with not a few, it is desirable to know if priests and deacons ordained in this fashion and with this form are validly ordained." It is to this question that the supposed decree of April 9, 1704, is a reply.

1 See the *Acts* of the Congregations (Thursday) held in presence of His Holiness, February 14, and April 10, 1704. Archives of the Holy Office, fasc. XIII. fol. 140 and foll.

Thus what our adversaries call a *decree* of the Holy See, and are pleased to oppose as a decisive argument to the august word of Leo XIII., was nothing more than a simple *votum* which in the point concerning the priesthood has no more value than what derives to it from the name of its obscure author. But, be its value great or little, in no way does it help the Anglican cause, since its true meaning is not that the sole three words—*Accipe Spiritum Sanctum*—constituted the adequate form of Coptic ordinations; but only that in certain cases they were an essential element, or, better still, a complement of that form. What these cases were which then and afterwards gave rise to doubt as to the validity of certain orders conferred with the Coptic rite is clearly stated in an ancient *Relation*,[1] sent to the Supreme Congregation by the Prefect Apostolic of the Copts. "When there are many to be ordained," says the *Relation*, "for instance, twenty or thirty, the Bishop does not lay his hand upon the head of all, but holds it stretched out a little above their heads without touching them, and recites the form for all together;[2] then, before giving them the Communion in both kinds, *he puts his two hands upon the two cheeks of each* and blows three times upon their face and mouth, and says in Coptic: *Ci imbneuma csuab, i. e., Accipe Spiritum Sanctum.*

The doubt therefore had reference to the case of *collective* ordinations, when, to supply any defect there might be in application to each of the matter and form laid down in the Coptic Pontifical, the ceremony above described was added for each individual in particular.

[1] Archives of the Holy Office. Fasc. XXIII., fol. 86-88.

[2] In the case to which an answer was given by the Consultor Damasceno, it is supposed that *at times there were three or four thousand or more in one day.*

Therefore, the second supposition of the Anglicans is also false; namely, that in this ceremony alone and in the sole three words repeated for every candidate, was found the *whole* rite, the *adequate* form, of those Coptic ordinations, pronounced valid by the Consultor Damasceno.[1]

The *defectus formae* that caused Leo XIII. to declare the insufficiency of the Edwardine Ordinal, far from being obscured, is brought out into clearer light, if we compare the Anglican form with the genuine Coptic Pontifical: for whilst, as is notorious, in the former there is no express indication of the order or power to be conferred, in the latter they are found more clearly and explicitly determined than in any of the liturgical forms already quoted. For example, let us take the form for priesthood as recorded among the *Acts* of the Holy Office, in the *votum* drawn up by the learned Assemani, in 1773: "The Bishop facing the west lays his right

---

[1] Cardinal Franzelin, in 1875, a year before he was created Cardinal, at the time Consultor of the Supreme Congregation, made a learned and deep study of the above mentioned controversy. We give here his conclusion, referred to by the London *Tablet*, Nov. 21, 1896, p. 805; "From all the discussions, hitherto had, it seems to be clear that the supposed Resolution of 1704 was never ratified by a Decree of the Sacred Congregation, but that it was merely a *votum* of the Consultor; that the Sacred Congregation in 1860 made use of it for *that part only* of which there was then question, namely, concerning the invalidity of the Ordinations, in which not the imposition of the hands of the Bishop but only of the Patriarchal cross is said to be used; that, moreover, from the Coptic rite handed down from ancient times, as may be seen in their Pontifical books, it is manifest that the words, *Receive the Holy Ghost*, do not constitute the whole form; that the Sacred Congregation never explicitly nor implicitly declared that only these words, with the imposition of hands, sufficed for validly conferring the Order of Priesthood." *Votum datum Romae, die 25 Feb., 1875.* Arch. of S. Office. Cf. the answer of Card. Patrizi, April 30, 1875, to Card. Manning. The text of this answer is quoted by *Gasparri, Tract. Can. de Sac. Ord.* No. 1058. See also *De Hierarchia Anglicana, p. 248.*

hand on the candidate and prays thus: Lord God our Ruler . . . look upon N., thy servant who is to be promoted to the priesthood on the testimony of those who have presented him ; *fill him with the Holy Ghost*, with the spirit of grace and counsel, that he may fear Thee and *rule Thy people* with a pure heart . . . Grant him the spirit of Thy wisdom, that full of works *unto healing* and words *unto teaching*, he may instruct Thy people in meekness . . . that he may *perform the office of a priest over Thy people*, and *renew with the laver of regeneration* as many as draw nigh unto him. (Here signing his brow with the thumb, he says:) We call thee, N. *as a priest to the Holy Altar of the Faithful* in the name of the Father, and of the Son, and of the Holy Ghost. Amen."

The Prayer "Omnipotens Deus."

In order to remedy the evident defect proper to the vague and imperative forms of the Edwardine Ordinal, some defenders of the validity of Anglican Orders have recourse to the prayer *Omnipotens Deus*, which is read after the Litany, maintaining that the true, sufficient and valid form is not found only in the words *Accipe Spiritum Sanctum*, but in them together with this prayer. To prove their assumption they insist on the moral union which exists between all the parts of the Anglican rite, and therefore between the prayer referred to and the imposition of hands later on, although there is between them a considerable interval during which many other ceremonies take place. But even prescinding from the question whether the sacramental form can in this way precede its proximate matter, it is plain that the pretended moral union then only is sufficient when the two parts morally united are both *essential*

parts of the same sacramental rite; now can we say that the prayer *Omnipotens Deus* is no less an essential part of the Edwardine Ordination rite than the laying-on of hands with the words: *Accipe Spiritum Sanctum?* Were it so, it ought to be recited by the consecrating Bishop; but this is not prescribed in the rubric; and moreover it is a well-attested fact, that, in past times at least, it was said indifferently by the consecrator or by someone else. Further; the essential part of a rite cannot be found outside it; but this prayer in the Edwardine Ordinal in use from 1662 till now is found *outside* the rite for ordaining deacons and priests. It is read, and according to the rubric ought to be read, as a Collect in the so-called Communion-service, which is distinct from the ordination-service. Hence Abbé Boudinhon, a witness not unfavorable to Anglicans, was forced to observe that: "This indeed constitutes a serious difficulty, ... it is certainly strange to find the essential ordination prayer in the collect of the mass; the mass and the ordination are two distinct liturgical functions ... one can hardly presume that the prelate in reciting the collect intends to confer ordination."[1]

Moreover, it must be observed that, in the very case of consecrating a bishop, the prayer in question is recited when, according to the Ordinal, the rite of consecration strictly so called has not yet begun. The Anglican rubric on this point is unmistakable. Here is what it says immediately after that prayer: "Then the Archbishop sitting in his chair shall say to him that is to be consecrated: Brother, forasmuch as the Holy

---

[1] "Ceci constitue déjà une sérieuse difficulté. . . . Il y a plus, quelque chose de bien étrange à voir la prière essentielle de l'ordination dans la collecte de la messe; la messe et l'ordination sont deux fonctions liturgiques . . . . l'on ne saurait présumer que le prélat, récitant la collecte, veuille faire l'ordination." *Revue Anglo-Romaine*, July 14, 1896, p. 676.

Scripture and the ancient canons command that we should not be hasty in laying on hands, and admitting any person to government in the Church of Christ which he hath purchased with no less price than the effusion of his own blood; BEFORE I admit *you to this administration* I will examine you in certain articles," etc.

Thereupon follows a lengthy examination consisting of eight questions put by the consecrator to him who is to be consecrated, and as the latter is free to answer any of them negatively he is still in a position to be dismissed. After this examination has been gone through to the satisfaction of both parties, another prayer is said; and then only does the rite of consecration strictly so called begin, with the singing or recitation of the *Veni Creator*. Then there is more prayer, and at last we come to the laying-on of hands with the words *Accipe Spiritum Sanctum*. From all this it is clear, not merely that the laying-on of hands, or the *matter* of the Sacrament, is separated by a long interval from that prayer in which our opponents would find at least a part of the form for episcopal ordination; but also that this supposed precatory form is placed outside the rite of consecration, and is therefore separated from the matter *morally* as well as physically. No wonder that their opinion, as they themselves allow,[1] was never admitted nor even known by the compilers of the Ordinal; no wonder that those very Anglicans who have recently defended the cause of their own Orders at Rome have

---

[1] Mgr. Gasparri, in his work *De la Valeur des Ordinations Anglicanes*, discussing this point, which he adopts, confesses that "the Anglicans, even the Compilers of the Ordinal, did not think of it," (les Anglicans, même les redacteurs de l'Ordinal, n'y avaient pas pensé), and subjoins, "According to others, the form consists in the words: '*Accipe Spiritum Sanctum.*' Such, no doubt, was the opinion of the compilers of the Ordinal," p. 45. note 2.

Defect of Form and Intention.

always adhered and do still firmly adhere to the opposite opinion.[1]

For the rest, although we were to admit a moral union between the prayer *Omnipotens Deus*, where the order to be conferred is mentioned, and the subsequent laying-on of hands; and even if we were to suppose a like mention in all the rubrics and prayers prescribed by the *Ordinal*, still there would always remain the principal flaw which vitiates the form—namely, that, *id reticet quod deberet proprium significare*, it says nothing of what it ought particularly to specify; nothing of *priesthood* in the strict sense as instituted by Christ at the Last Supper, when He said to His Apostles: "Do this for a commemoration of Me." For as a matter of fact, as we have already seen, the *Ordinal* was substituted for the ancient Catholic Pontifical with the explicit, deliberate and firm resolve of excluding every idea of priesthood from the Anglican Church; and, to this end, its compilers not only denied the existence of the Sacrament of Orders, but of set purpose left out, changed or mutilated all those ancient formulas and ceremonies which in any way asserted or supposed or symbolized the priesthood, the Real Presence, or the Eucharistic Sacrifice. And, therefore, the words *bishop* and *priest* which occur here and there in the Anglican *Ordinal* are, as the Bull rightly observes, mere names meaning something different from the reality instituted by Christ[2]—*restant nomina sine re quam instituit Christus.*

---

[1] Mr. Lacey wrote thus, a few days before the publication of the Bull of Leo XIII.: "In our dissertation, my confrère, Edward Denny, and I, according to our ability, contend that the imperative formulas, which are used in the Anglican Ordinations, be considered as *valid and adequate forms* joined with the imposition of hands. *Neither will depart from this opinion.*" Op. cit. p. 19.

[2] Over-seer, elder, servant, by force of their *etymology—i.e*, episcopus, presbyter, diaconus—have no "sacerdotalist" meaning,

Dr. Taylor, Anglican Archdeacon of Liverpool, confirms what has been just said.[1] "It is a simple matter of historical fact that, in the *Ordinal* of 1550, not only was the *sacrificial* formula of ordaining (*Receive the power of offering sacrifice*, a. s. f.) expunged, but every other trace of the sacerdotal and sacrificial idea was deliberately, and of set purpose, removed and wholly eliminated from it. The word 'priest' is indeed retained, but the priestly functions and expressions are gone." Dr. Ryle, also an Anglican and Bishop of Liverpool, reasserts the same fact. "Our manner of conceiving the office of a minister of Christ is very different from that of the Pope. On the one hand, the ecclesiastic of the Roman Church is a true Priest, whose principal duty is to offer the sacrifice of the Mass. On the other hand, the ecclesiastic of the Anglican Church is in no wise a Priest, *although we call him such;* he is only an Elder, whose principal office is not to offer a sacrifice, but rather to preach the word of God and to administer the Sacraments."[2]

The Defect of Due Intention.

But, as we said at the beginning, the essential defectiveness of the form is not the only ground of complaint, for there is besides the defect of due intention which is closely connected with it.

This due intention, as is well known, is absolutely necessary for the validity of all the Sacraments. "If any man say that an intention at least of doing what the Church does is not required in the ministers when they make or confer the Sacraments, let him be anath-

---

and as such could be well retained as names of official grades in the ecclesiastical polity of a body whose desire was to retain the shadow and part with the substance of the Catholic religion.

1 *Tablet,* Nov. 7, 1896.
2 The *Guardian,* Nov. 4, 1896, p. 1766.

Defect of Form and Intention. 105

ema." Thus the Council of Trent defines; thus the leading Anglican canonists[1] teach; thus the very nature of that "human act," whereby the Church's minister must perform the rite prescribed by her, requires that it should be.[2]

As the Bull states explicitly, the Church can only judge of the existence of this intention so far as it is outwardly manifested; as to the mind or intention, so far as it is something hidden within, the Church passes no judgment; but so far as it is declared outwardly she ought to judge of it. Therefore the Church holds, and till the contrary is proved wishes all to hold, that such due intention is never absent whensoever the minister seriously goes through the sacramental rite she has prescribed, using the matter and form which she uses. For this reason, while the Church has never recognized the validity of Sacraments administered by fools or in a state of drunkenness or in jest, yet she has always admitted that baptism conferred by a heretic or even by a pagan, provided it has been proved *in foro externo* that the proximate matter, together with the due form, had

---

1 O. J. REICHEL, *A Complete Manual of Canon Law*, London, 1896, pp. 11, 12.

2 "A lifeless instrument has no *intention* with regard to the effect it produces, the impulse it receives from him who uses it supplying the place of intention. But a living instrument, like the minister of a Sacrament, is not merely impelled, but to a certain extent impels itself, inasmuch as it puts its members into action by its will; and hence an intention is required on its part whereby it subjects itself to the principal agent, so as to intend to do what Christ and the Church does." (Aquinas, Summa, iii. 64, 8 ad 1.) In other words, we must distinguish between the man and the minister. It is in many other matters, too, that a mere intention determines whether one is acting officially or unofficially. It does not matter that the minister believes or disbelieves concerning the Church or the Sacrament; all that is requisite is the intention of acting officially as the Church's minister. By that intention he, so to say, puts himself into the Church's hand and it is she who, as principal agent, uses his words and acts as her instruments for conferring sacramental grace.

been seriously applied. For the same reason the Church has never doubted the validity of ordinations conferred by criminal, or heretical, or schismatical bishops, but had allowed the orders of Nestorians, Monophysites and other Eastern schismatics. For in all such cases, as St. Thomas says, the minister of the Sacrament, by the very fact of deliberately and seriously using the rite approved by the Church, is reasonably presumed to be acting as her representative; "in the words which he utters," being the Church's own words, "the intention of the Church herself is expressed, which suffices for the performance of the Sacrament, unless the contrary be outwardly expressed."

But if the heretical minister of the Sacrament, in order to maintain his particular heresy, of set purpose corrupts or rejects the Catholic rite, and in the administration of the Sacrament uses a *new* form, which *excludes* the signification of the Catholic forms, can such a minister be supposed to have the intention required for validity, namely, "of at least doing what the Church does?"

Such, in short, is the question to be dealt with in discussing the validity of Orders conferred by Anglican bishops with the new rite of Edward VI.

The Judgment of Former Popes.

Put thus, the question admits only of the negative answer given to it by Julius III. in 1553-4; by Paul IV. in 1555; by Clement XI. in 1704, and, of late, by Leo XIII. in his Bull of September 8, 1896: "If the rite is changed for the express purpose of bringing in another not received by the Church and of exchanging what the Church does and what belongs to the nature of the Sacrament by the institution of Christ, then manifestly not only is the intention absent which is requisite

for the Sacrament, but a contrary and repugnant intention is present."

The doctrine here stated so clearly by the reigning Pope was enunciated with just as much precision by his predecessor Pope Zachary, in 746. The latter was informed by two illustrious ecclesiastics, Virginius and Sidonius[1], that a certain priest of their province through his ignorance of Latin[2] used, when baptizing, to mangle the form, saying: "Baptizo te in nomine Patria et Filia et Spiritus Sancti," and that S. Boniface, Archbishop of Mayence, deeming such baptism invalid, had ordered them to rebaptize all who had been baptized by the same priest in the manner aforesaid.

Upon this, Pope Zachary wrote the famous letter to S. Boniface, dated July 1, 748, and set the Decree of Gratian[3]: "Most Holy Brother: if he who baptized them spoke as above, not for the sake of introducing error or heresy but marring the language simply through ignorance of the Roman diction, we cannot consent to their being rebaptized[4]." Therefore the Pope recognized that if the said corruption had been effected, not by mere ignorance of the language, but by a deliberate purpose of introducing error or heresy, the Sacrament would certainly be invalid; in other words, that in the latter hypothesis the change would have been a proof that in using a corrupt sacramental form he did not

[1] Both became Bishops afterwards, Virginius of Salzburg, and Sidonius of Passau. *Cf. P. JAFFÉ, Monumenta Moguntina,* Berlin, 1866. p. 167, notes 3 and 4.

[2] "Dum baptizaret, nesciens latini eloquii, infringens linguam."

[3] Part III. *De Consecratione,* Dist. IV, can. 86. The text cited by us is that published by *JAFFÉ* in his *Bibliotheca Rerum Germanicarum,* Tom. III, *as above,* p. 168.

[4] "Sanctissime frater, si ille qui baptizavit *non errorem introducens aut haeresim,* sed, pro sola ignorantia romanæ locutionis infringendo linguam, ut supra fati sumus, dixisset, non possumus consentire ut denuo baptizentur."

intend to do through it what the Church does through her form.

THE CHANGE OF WORDS.

So it is that S. Thomas, the faithful interpreter of Catholic tradition reasons, speaking of the validity of the sacramental form when the fixed words of which it consists are corrupted in the pronunciation, he distinguishes carefully, as Pope Zachary had already done, between cases where it happens through ignorance and those where it is deliberately effected. Of the latter cases he writes: "He who corrupts the sacramental words in the pronunciation, if he does it of set purpose, is shown not to intend to do what the Church does, and therefore is shown not to perform the Sacrament."[1] Afterwards, dealing expressly with our present question, namely, whether, saving the validity of the Sacrament, it is possible to change the form by an addition or subtraction, he teaches that: "As touching all these changes which may come about in the sacramental forms, two things are to be considered; the first, in regard to him who pronounces the words, whose intention is necessary for the Sacrament; and if therefore, by such addition or subtraction, he intends to introduce another rite which is not received by the Church, the Sacrament is shown not to be valid, because he appears not to intend to do what the Church does."[2]

[1] Dicendum, quod ille qui corrupte profert verba sacramentalia, *si hoc ex industria facit*, non videtur intendere facere quod facit Ecclesia; et ita non videtur perfici sacramentum."—*Summa Theologica*, P. III, quæst. 60. art. 7. ad 3.

[2] "Circa omnes istas mutationes quae possunt in formis sacramentorum contingere, duo videntur esse consideranda: unum quidem ex parte eius qui profert verba cuius intentio requiritur ad sacramentum; et ideo *si intendat*, per huiusmodi additionem vel diminutionem, *alium ritum inducere qui non sit ab Ecclesia receptus*, non videtur perfici sacramentum; quia *non videtur, quod intendat facere id quod facit Ecclesia.*" Ibid, art. 8. *Respondeo dicendum*.

And Gasparri[1] himself admits that the most illustrious theologians have always argued in the same way. Cardinal DeLugo,[2] for instance, among the older, and Cardinal D'Annibale among the more recent. The latter says: "What some teach as to the invalidity of a Sacrament when the minister makes some non-substantial change," (*a fortiori* if it be substantial), "with a view to introducing an error or new rite, is to be understood as implying that he is thought not to have the intention of doing what the Church does. It is a question, therefore, of presumption; of *fact* and not of *law*."

The full justification of this presumption is not plain till we remember that, in the sacramental forms, we should attend not merely to the words considered *materially*, e. g., whether they be grammatically masculine or feminine, or whether they can be understood in this sense or another; but we must attend also, and even principally to the special, and, so to say, concrete sense given to them by him who pronounces them. Whenever, therefore, such words, according to the minister's ordinary use of the language, and having regard to the end for which they were introduced and employed by him, have a signification evidently opposite to that always given them by the Church, it can safely be said that the minister in question wishes to do the *opposite* to what the Church does; but he can never be supposed to wish to do the *same* thing.

[1] *De la valeur des Ordinations Anglicanes*, Paris, 1895, p. 25.

[2] *De Sacramentis in genere*, Disp. II, no. 116. Lyons, 1670, p. 32. There *DE LUGO* correctly observes that, "St. Thomas does not universally deny the validity of a Sacrament administered with the intention of introducing a *new* rite, but he infers by argument the probable defect of the requisite intention." ("St. Thomas non negat universaliter valorem Sacramenti cum intentione inducendi *novum* ritum, sed arguitive infert probabiliter defectum debitae intentionis.") That is true only with reference to the *novelty* of the rite, not when there is question of a *signification opposed* to the Catholic rite.

The Intention of the Reformers.

Now this and nothing else is what we find in regard to the Orders conferred by the Edwardine *Ordinal*. That this *Ordinal*, compiled by notorious heretics and substituted by lay authority for the Catholic Pontifical, differs from the Pontifical, is a fact admitted by all.[1] Further: no one has ever been bold enough to deny that it differs from all the other ancient Pontificals of East and West recognized as valid by the Church, and preserved even still by heretics and schismatics; and we ourselves have already given abundant proof of the same. Also, because among these various rites none corresponded to the taste and intentions of the English Reformers, they resolved to take no account of them, and to introduce a *new* Ordinal, which they accordingly did.[2]

Furthermore, it is beyond doubt that all liturgical innovations, and especially those in the rite of ordination, were made by the compilers of the *Ordinal*, not casually or through error or ignorance, but of set purpose, with the deliberate intention of excluding from the new forms whatever was found in the old ones to be repugnant or opposed to the doctrines which they professed.[3]

And thus the English reformers, who repudiated the

1 Cf. *G. W. CHILD, Church and State under the Tudors*, London, 1879. pp. 114-117; *ESTCOURT, The Question of Anglican Ordinations Discussed*, London, 1873, *passim*.

2 Since the change was presumably not for nothing, but either to eliminate some popish error or to introduce some neglected essential, we may ask Anglicans to state clearly what was the advantage directly aimed at, if it was not to exclude all notion of a sacrificing priesthood?

3 See *DOM GASQUET, Edward VI. and the Book of Common Prayer*, pp. 261 and foll.; *N. POCOCK, The Principles of the Reformation*, etc. London, 1875, pp. 12 and 19; *The English History Review*, October, 1886.

Catholic doctrine as to the existence and nature of the Sacrament of Orders, as their acts and writings attest,[1] strove for this very reason, *i. e.*, to admit any necessary *form* or *matter* would have been inconsistent with the explicit denial of a *Sacrament* of Orders—to suppress all mention in the consecratory forms of the order or power to be conferred; whence originates that vagueness and indefiniteness in the forms already adverted to. But that this fundamental error was not simply a private one in their own mind, but was also publicly professed by them, is proved not only from the witness of contemporary English writers, but also from the explicit declaration of the 25th of those Anglican *Articles*, which were compiled and substituted for the profession of the Catholic faith at the same time that the new Ordinal was compiled and substituted for the Catholic Pontifical. It runs as follows: "*There are two sacraments ordained of Christ our Lord in the Gospel, that is to say, Baptism and the Supper of the Lord. Those five commonly called Sacraments, that is to say, Confirmation, Penance, Orders, Matrimony and Extreme Unction, are not to be counted for Sacraments of the Gospel, being such as have grown partly of the corrupt following of the Apostles; partly, are states of life allowed in the Scriptures, but yet have not like nature of Sacraments with Baptism and the Lord's Supper, for they have not any visible sign or ceremony ordained of God.*"[2]

[1] BURNET, *History of the Reformation;* vol. I, page 461, and vol. IV, page 471; HUNT, *Religious Thought in England*, vol. I, p. 43. Cf. CHILD *op. cit.* Appendix pp. 293-304. A full collection of the opinions of the compilers of the Ordinal was prepared for the use of the Roman Commission by the English theologians MOYES, GASQUET and DAVID FLEMING. We were able to consult it, and verify the accuracy of the assertion made in the text.

[2] In the Catholic Pontifical used in England before the reform of Edward VI., the candidate for Priesthood is admonished that those who are to be ordained "receive the chalice with wine, and the paten

It was only natural that as they denied the Sacrament of Orders to be a true sacrament the compilers of the new Ordinal should also deny the dogmas so closely bound up with it, such as the Real Presence, the sacrificing priesthood, the Sacrifice of the Altar. And so they excluded the Mass from their new Liturgy; declaring that: "the sacrifices of Masses, in which it was commonly said that the priest did offer Christ for the quick and the dead to have remission of pain or guilt, were blasphemous fables and dangerous deceits." (Article XXXI.)

Hence they eliminated from their Ordinal all those ceremonies which supposed or referred to any of the said dogmas, such as the consecration with sacred oils, the giving of the instruments,[1] and the rest. Whoever will take the trouble to compare the Pontifical with the Edwardine rite of ordination will see at a glance how studiously the latter has avoided all mention of priesthood, priest, sacrifice and altar; and how systematically the formulas and prayers have been mutilated, adulterated or altogether suppressed, wherever they make any reference to those things which the Church has always and everywhere desired to express by them.

And, therefore, to pretend that the Anglican bishop ordaining with this new rite of his, which is the direct negation of the Catholic rite, means to do what the

---

with hosts from the hand of the Bishop, inasmuch as by these instruments *they may know that they have received the power of offering propitiatory victims to God; for to them it belongs to celebrate the Sacrament of the Body and Blood of the Lord on the Altar of God.*" ("Accipiunt et calicem cum vino et patenam cum hostiis de manu Episcopi, quatenus his instrumentis, *potestatem se accepisse agnoscant placabiles Deo hostias offerendi: Ad ipsos namque pertinet saramentum Corporis et Sanguinis Domini in Altare Dei conficere.*")

1 See on this point the excellent work of Rev. Sidney F. Smith, *Reasons for Rejecting Anglican Orders*. London, 1895, pp. 69 and foll.

Defect of Form and Intention.

Church does with her rite, would be to pretend that two forms, not merely different, but opposite in their signification, could produce the same formal effect.

THE INTENTION OF THE CHURCH.

And, in fine, what is it that the Church intends and has always, both in East and West, intended, in conferring Holy Orders on her ministers? If we study her express declarations, and especially her liturgies, it is clear that she intends and has always intended to do what Christ did at the Last Supper—namely, to make true *priests*, who should not merely have power to preach the Word of God and to administer the Sacraments, but who should also be gifted with the visible and external priesthood, instituted by the same Christ Our Lord, for the purpose of consecrating and offering upon the altar His very Body and Blood, under the appearances of bread and wine.

"Christ," says the Council of Trent, "declaring himself to be constituted a priest forever after the order of Melchisedech, offered his Body and Blood to God the Father, under the appearances of bread and wine, and gave them under the same sign to His apostles, whom He then was making priests of the New Testament, that they might eat thereof; and He commanded that they and their successors in the priesthood should offer the same, saying, 'Do this for a commemoration of Me,' as the Catholic Church has always understood and taught."[1] And are we to suppose that this is what the compilers of the Ordinal intended, and what the Anglican bishops intended, and intend to do when they consecrate and ordain with the said Ordinal? If so, why did the former of set purpose change the ancient

[1] Conc. Trid. Dec. de sac. missae, Sess. XXII. c. 1.

rite wherever there was reference to priesthood; and why do the latter deliberately make use of the forms so changed? Why have they abandoned the Catholic Pontifical and all the ancient rites to introduce and use continually a new rite not received by the Church?

The answer is clear. They did so and do so because they have positively excluded priesthood in the strict sense. By those forms and with that rite it is their intention to constitute simply a minister who *may be called* Presbyter or Bishop; but never has it been their intention to make a true *priest* (*sacerdos*). And this the genuine Anglican, who is not a ritualist, confesses openly and honestly.

A writer in the *Speaker* says:[1] "The majority of English Anglicans never supposed that their clergy possessed the powers peculiar to the Roman Catholic priesthood, and they have always repulsed every pretension of authority founded on such sacerdotal power." Another writer:[2] "With the reformation the heads of the Church of England separated deliberately and effectively from the Church of Rome, repudiated her teaching on the Priesthood and Episcopate, *and therefore, never had, in ordaining, any intention of conferring a priesthood*, since they considered *sacerdotalism* an injury to the priesthood of Christ, without foundation in Scripture, and repugnant to all the cardinal doctrines of the Gospel." A third adds:[3] "The ecclesiastic in the Church of Rome is *a true priest*, whose principal office is to offer the Sacrifice of the Mass." On the other hand, the ecclesiastic in the Anglican Church is *in no manner a priest*, although he is so called; he is only a

[1] September 26, 1896.
[2] The *Rock*, September 25, 1896.
[3] DR. RYLE, Anglican Bishop of Liverpool, in the *Guardian*, November 4, 1896.

Presbyter." A fourth states:[1] "We do not believe in Orders in the Catholic sense. . . . Do what we will, we *cannot* offer sacrifices. *We are only ministers*, like our brethren in the Nonconformist churches."

THIS INTENTION EXCLUDED FROM THE EDWARDINE ORDINAL.

With good reason, then, did H. E. Cardinal Vaughan write recently to an Anglican: "It is impossible to ignore the doctrinal and historical fact that for three centuries the Church of England has repudiated the essential character of the Catholic rite of ordination, and has used instead a form which was of set purpose intended to exclude the idea of a sacrificing priesthood."[2]

To say, therefore, what some have said lately, that he who ordains in conformity with the Ordinal of Edward VI., seriously intends thereby to make true *priests* such as the Church has always made, is an outrage on common sense.[3] Whence Franzelin[4] wisely observes: "Since the Sacraments of the New Law are *visible effectual signs*, they effect just what they signify. It is, then, absurd that a visible rite *from which the signification*

---

[1] The Vicar of Hexton, in the *Echo*, quoted by the *Tablet*, December 19, 1896, p. 975.

[2] Letter to Mr. Howell, October 2, 1894. See *The Tablet* of Oct. 13, 1894, p. 581.

[3] The same must be said of the assertion of those who pretend that the compilers of the *Ordinal*, by abolishing the Priesthood and the Sacrifice, and by rejecting the ancient rites for a new one which would correspond to their heresy, desired merely to restore the rite of Ordination to its primitive institution of Apostolic times.

[4] "Cum sacramenta novae legis sint *visibilia signa efficacia*, illud operantur quod significant: absurdum ergo est, ritum visibilem *in quo excluditur significatio potestatis sacerdotalis* conferendae, esse sacramentum ad hanc ipsam potestatem conferendam. *Votum* of February 25, 1875, p. 9, Archives of the Holy Office."

of priestly power is excluded, should be a Sacrament for the conferring of priestly power.

Mr. Lacey's Vicious Circle.

From what has been said so far, it will be easy to see the emptiness of the accusation which Mr. Lacey makes against the Bull of Leo XIII., in the *Contemporary Review* for December, 1896. According to him, the doctrinal portion of the Bull revolves within the narrow limits of the vicious circle, proving the invalidity of the form from the defect of due intention, and the defect of due intention from the invalidity of the form; so that "the two arguments combined will make an excellent circle. Read apart, they leave us wondering what the Bull does mean."

Whatever be true of other readers we are certain that at least Mr. Lacey and his ritualistic colleagues, who worked so hard to hinder[1] the publication of the Bull, are perfectly clear as to "what it does mean;" and perhaps it is just because its meaning is so clear and peremptory that they are so anxious by cavillings and sophisms to find obscurities in it. Be that as it may, the accusation made by Mr. Lacey is absolutely unfounded, since neither is the invalidity of the form proved from the defect of intention, nor conversely. The invalidity of the Anglican form is demonstrated from the fact that the said form, considered in itself and in the historical circumstances which determined its compilation, is vague and indefinite; it lacks the principal essential elements common to all Catholic forms; it makes

[1] Note what we have said of the actions of Messrs. Lacey and Puller in Rome, *on page 46, note.* To become convinced of the facts one need but read Mr. Lacey's statements in his article, regarding his relations with several of the Cardinals and two members of the Roman Commission.

no mention of what from its very nature the sacramental form of Ordination should signify. Into all this the heretical intention of the minister who makes use of the form in no way enters. The form would be and would remain invalid although the Anglican minister wished thereby to effect what the Catholic Church effects with her form.

In like manner the defect of due intention in the Anglican minister is not deduced from the simple fact that he uses an invalid form in ordaining, but from the fact, so often insisted on, that in conforming himself seriously to the Ordinal, he makes use of a form which he knows was changed of set purpose, and substituted deliberately for that of the Catholic Pontifical, with a view to introducing a new rite, different from and in its adequate signification opposite not only to that of the Church of Rome, but also to those of all the Churches East and West, from the remotest antiquity even to our own days. If Mr. Lacey will read the Bull again, with a little more attention, he will perhaps be convinced of the great blunder he has committed.

THE "HISTORICAL ERROR" ON THE OTHER SIDE.

There is another accusation of Mr. Lacey's in the said article which we must not let pass unblamed. He accuses the Holy Father of having committed "an extraordinary blunder" in his Bull by asserting that in 1704 the practice to be followed, when the *Traditio instrumentorum* had been omitted in ordination, was already established.

Before examining the proof with which Mr. Lacey substantiates his accusation, it will be well to notice that the statement in the Bull which he refers to is founded on a number of decisions given by the Holy Office previous to 1704; decisions which if published

along with their accompanying *acts* and *votes* would almost fill two great folio volumes. Elsewhere we gave an indication of the existence of these documents with their precise dates (1603-1699), and of the general title under which they are found collected together and preserved in the archives of the Holy Office. Here, for example is one, of 1697. Mgr. Scanagatta, Bishop of Avellino, suffering from gout in the hands, had omitted for some time in ordinations the customary *traditio instrumentorum* prescribed by the Pontifical. When this got to be known by Cardinal Orsini, then Archbishop of Benevento, afterwards Pope Benedict XIII., he referred the case to the Congregation of the Holy Office asking, as we read in the *Acts:* "Not indeed if the ordinations are to be repeated, but only as to the mode of ordaining, whether it is to be repeated absolutely or conditionally." The inquiry was answered by the following decree: "On Wednesday, August 1, 1697, the doubt was again proposed and thoroughly discussed as to whether the ordinations performed by the Bishop of Avellino are null and void for that he did not himself deliver the instruments, or matter, of the subdiaconate, diaconate and priesthood, respectively; and also, whether the aforesaid, who have been ordained in Holy Orders, are to be absolutely ordained or only under condition; His Holiness (Innocent XIII.) having heard, etc., *decreed* that in the case in question it was safer that the ordinations should be reiterated under condition." This decree is seven years earlier than that issued in 1704 by Clement XI. in the case of the Anglican Bishop Gordon, and is, as we have said, one of a long series of like decrees published by the same Congregation of the Holy Office during the whole century preceding 1704. There is no doubt, therefore, of the absolute exactness and historical truth of Leo XIII.'s assertion that at the time of Clement XI., and particularly in 1704, when the

Defect of Form and Intention. 119

"giving of instruments" was omitted, "it was customarily prescribed that the ordination should be repeated under condition."

Whence it follows that the "extraordinary blunder" has been committed not by him who on the faith of so many weighty documents has asserted the fact, but by him who has denied it,[1] ignoring and not even suspecting the existence of such document.

The "Extraordinary Blunder."

But the "blunder" seems still more "extraordinary" when we examine the proof Mr. Lacey[2] offers in order to convict the Bull of an historical error. The whole of this proof consists of a *Resolution* of the Congregation of the Council, dated later than 1704, and quoted by Benedict XIV.[3] In this *Resolution*, it is enjoined that *verificatis expositis, i c*, the omission of the delivery of the instruments being proved, "let the bishop proceed[4] to repeat the whole ordination in private, under condition." In order to use this as a proof of his thesis against the Bull, we must suppose, as Mr. Lacey sup-

---

[1] Mr. Lacey might have been more cautious in making his accusation against the Pontiff if he had consulted the work, known to him, of *P. LE QUIEN, Nullité des Ordinations Anglicanes*, Paris, Simart, 1725. In it(Tom. ii, p.390) is found the case of Mgr. Du Moulinet, Bishop of Seez, who, as in the instance cited by us above, had omitted in the Ordinations the tradition of the instruments. The solution given in *1604* by Pope Clement VIII.*of repeating the ordination conditionally*, is found in the letters there transcribed by the Secretary of Cardinal Bubalis, Nuncio in France.

[2] *Contemporary Review*, p. 799.

[3] *De Synodo Dioecesana*, lib. viii, cap. 10, Tom. xi, 1854, pp. 268-272.

[4] *Ut verificatis expositis, Episcopus procedat ad secreto iterandam ordinationem ex integro sub conditione.* The identical solution was repeated in 1796. See *Lib. Decret.* 146, Arch. of the Congregation of the Council

poses, that this *resolution* was absolutely *the first*[1] of its kind ever sanctioned by the Church. Now, this is proved clearly false by the documents of the Holy Office, cited above. But neither can it be supposed with truth that it was the first, in a relative sense, among a series of similar decisions given by the same Congregation of the Council. In fact, the *Acts* of that tribunal, which Mr. Lacey seems to mix up with the Holy Office, openly attest the contrary. According to the *Raccolta* lately published by Pallottini,[2] the said *resolution* seems to have been preceded by at least three or four others of the same tenor. And in this, also, the Congregation of the Council had simply considered what was the ancient practice, and had guided its own action by that of the Supreme Congregation of the Holy Office in past years.

Conclusion.

The Holy Father assures us that before giving his final judgment on the intrinsic worth of Anglican Ordinations he desired that all the arguments for them should be examined accurately, and particularly by Himself in union with their Eminencies, the Judges of the Supreme Congregation, and especially those arguments which had been discussed *pro* and *con* by able theologians, canonists and historians in a special Roman Commission instituted by him expressly for this purpose. "All these things He and Our Venerable Brethren, the Judges of the Supreme Congregation, pondered long and deeply." Furthermore, the Holy Father wished before giving sentence to consider the question of opportuneness, " whether it was opportune and expedient that the

[1] *In the Contemporary Review*, p. 799, he takes this for granted, "*Such is the origin of the practice.*"

[2] Collectio omnium Conclus, et Resolut. Congreg. Concilii, etc. Tom. xvi., Roma, 1892, pp. 63-68.

Defect of Form and Intention. 121

same should be declared again by Our authority," thus satisfying the scruples of those who feared lest a new authoritative declaration might break off, or at least partly arrest, the happy reaction towards Catholicism observable for some time past in England. But in the present circumstances and after the fierce polemics raised during the last two years in favor of Anglican Orders, not only by Ritualists, but even by some Catholic writers, it was obvious and natural that if the Pope had kept silent "a pernicious error would have been occasioned to not a few who think that they can find the Sacrament of Orders and the fruit thereof where it does not exist;" and therefore concludes Leo XIII.: "It seemed good in Our Lord that We should pronounce sentence."

It is not therefore policy or any other motive of mere human prudence which has induced Leo XIII. to condemn Anglican Ordinations, but only the irresistible evidence of their nullity, and the imperative duty he owes to God and to souls redeemed by the Blood of Christ. Faithful to his office as Supreme Teacher and Father and Pastor of all Christians, he would not, and could not leave under so dangerous a delusion so many of his children who, albeit separated from him, are sincerely seeking the Kingdom of Christ in the unity of the faith.

Therefore, he has spoken, and his language has been clear, precise, and invested with all those attributes which plainly show his judgment to be not only a wise, just, and necessary act of the Highest authority in the Church, but also a perpetual, decisive and irrevocable act.[1]

[1] Mr. Lacey, in his article in the *Contemporary Review*, December, 1896, p. 803, grievously errs when he judges otherwise of the pronouncement by Leo XIII. against the validity of Anglican Ordinations. We are surprised and regret to find that the same error, fatal to numerous souls and repugnant to the text of the Bull and the intentions of the Holy Father, has been endorsed by the *Irish Ecclesiastical Record*, December, 1896, p. 1116.

Leo XIII. has struck a death-blow against the very essence of Anglican Orders, proving and declaring them null and void, through the intrinsic *defect of form and intention*. Thus Leo XIII. has shown that together with unity of doctrine, the Holy See preserves unity of language, as is strikingly illustrated and confirmed in the first part of the Bull from the acts of Julius III., Paul IV., and Clement XI.

It is the love of truth which has moved us to comment on this new document of Leo XIII. and to deal with a subject of such deep import, whether it be considered in itself and in regard to the British nation, which for political wisdom and power is the closest image of the ancient Roman Empire; or whether we take account of so many millions of souls which for three centuries have been living separated from the Church of Jesus Christ. If on the one hand the thought that so grand a people as the English, as it were naturally Christian, has been left for such cycles of years without the sacrifice of the altar and without a priesthood saddens and depresses us, yet the hope of seeing both restored to them once more together with that full and perfect submission to the See of Peter, which is essential to all religion, consoles us and spurs us on to do something for a cause to which we have already devoted years of diligent and affectionate study. It was in no sense party-spirit, or love of polemics and controversy, or any other less Christian motive which moved us to this enterprise, but only the reverence due to historical and theological truth, and the desire of serving a nation which the example of Leo XIII., and the holy memory of our English martyrs make it a duty for us to honor and love.

PONTIFICAL APPROBATION.

DILECTO FILIO SALVATORI BRANDI, E SOCIETATE
JESU, ROMAM,

LEO PP. XIII.,

Dilecte Fili, Salutem et Apostolicam Benedictionem.

Lucubrationibus ceteris, quibus ad hanc diem in adserenda veritate Ecclesiaeque maiestate vindicanda ingenium studiumque tuum probasti, aliam opportune admodum addidisti nuper qua sententiam Nostram de anglicanis ordinationibus, argumentis ex historia sacraque theologia petitis, illustrare ac tueri elaboras. Pergratae plane Nobis acciderunt industriae tuae ; quas eo maiori futuras utilitati novimus, quod libros a te conscriptos, in aliarum etiam gentium sermonem versos, edendos esse nunciasti. Consiliis laboribusque tuis benigne ut Deus obsecundet optamus. Ut vero paternae Nostrae dilectionis pignore solatioque ne careas, apostolicam tibi benedictionem amantissime in Domino impertimus.

Datum Romae apud S. Petrum, die XXII ianuarii MDCCCXCVII, Pontificatus Nostri anno decimo nono.

LEO PP. XIII.

TO OUR ESTEEMED SON, SALVATORE BRANDI, OF THE SOCIETY OF JESUS,

LEO PP. XIII.,

Health and Apostolic Benediction.

DEAR SON:—To other works, whereby up to the present you have shown your skill and readiness to set forth the teaching, and to champion the cause of Holy Church, you have latterly added a well-timed work, in which it has been your aim to illustrate and strengthen by arguments, historical and doctrinal, Our decision on Anglican Orders. Your efforts are indeed most gratifying to Us; all the more because We are sure they will redound to yet greater profit in that your books are to be circulated among other nations. May God graciously forward your plans and undertakings.

As an earnest of Our fatherly regard and for your spiritual comfort most lovingly in Our Lord do We bestow upon you the Apostolic Benediction.

Given at St. Peter's, at Rome, on the twenty-second day of January, 1897, in the nineteenth year of Our Pontificate.

LEO PP. XIII.

CONTENTS.

EDITOR'S PREFACE 2

THE BULL "APOSTOLICAE CURAE" (Latin and English) 4

COMMENTARY ON THE BULL "APOSTOLICAE CURAE."

    PART I. INTRODUCTORY 38

        Public Opinion in England regarding the Bull—English Protestants' view of same—The Ritualists—Disappointed—Historical Origin of the Anglican difficulty—Cranmer and the Anglican Ordinal—The Ordinal under Mary and Elizabeth—Modification introduced in the Rite—"Nag's Head" Story.

    PART II. THE JUDGMENT OF LEO XIII 57

        Reasons which prompted the Pontiff to pronounce the Orders Invalid—Julius III. and the early ordinations under the reign of Edward VI.—Paul IV. examines and decides the question in 1555—orders and benefices *nulliter et de facto*—The Bishop's "*rite et recte non ordinati*"—"*In forma Ecclesiae consueta*"—The foregoing interpretation confirmed by facts—The practice of reordaining Anglican Bishops and ministers since 1555—The case of John Gordon.

    PART III. DEFECT OF FORM AND INTENTION 83

        The ceremony and the essential rite of the Sacrament—The want of a specifically determined form—The different forms in the Liturgies of the Church—The conformity of the Edwardine Ordinal—Anglicans shifting the issue—No argument to be drawn from the Coptic rite—The prayer "*Omnipotens Deus*"—The defect of due intention—The judgment of former Popes—The change of words—Reformers' intention—The Church's intention—This intention excluded from the Edwardine Ordinal—Mr. Lacey's vicious circle—The historical error on the other side—The extraordinary blunder—Conclusion.

LETTER OF HIS HOLINESS APPROVING THE WORK . . . 124

www.ingramcontent.com/pod-product-compliance
Lightning Source LLC
Chambersburg PA
CBHW020114170426
43199CB00009B/529